T0320835

News Nerds

Oxford Studies in Digital Politics

Series Editor: Andrew Chadwick, Professor of Political Communication in the Centre for Research in Communication and Culture and the Department of Social Sciences, Loughborough University

News Nerds

INSTITUTIONAL CHANGE IN JOURNALISM

ALLIE KOSTERICH

Oxford University Press is a department of the University of Oxford. It furthers
the University's objective of excellence in research, scholarship, and education
by publishing worldwide. Oxford is a registered trade mark of Oxford University
Press in the UK and certain other countries.

Published in the United States of America by Oxford University Press
198 Madison Avenue, New York, NY 10016, United States of America.

© Oxford University Press 2022

Library of Congress Cataloging-in-Publication Data
Names: Kosterich, Allie, author.
Title: News nerds : institutional change in journalism / Allie Kosterich.
Description: New York : Oxford University Press, 2022. |
Series: Oxford studies digital politics series |
Includes bibliographical references and index.
Identifiers: LCCN 2022018972 (print) | LCCN 2022018973 (ebook) |
ISBN 9780197500354 (hardback) | ISBN 9780197500361 (paperback) |
ISBN 9780197500385 (epub) | ISBN 9780197500392
Subjects: LCSH: Journalism—Technological innovations. |
Journalism—Data processing. | Journalism—Social aspects. | Reporters and reporting.
Classification: LCC PN4784.T34 K67 2022 (print) |
LCC PN4784.T34 (ebook) | DDC 070.4/3—dc23
LC record available at https://lccn.loc.gov/2022018972
LC ebook record available at https://lccn.loc.gov/2022018973

DOI: 10.1093/oso/9780197500354.001.0001

For Anna Juliet

Contents

Acknowledgments

The seeds for this book were planted decades ago when my fascination with media evolved from an obsession with weekly newspaper comics to an appointment as editor-in-chief of my high school newspaper to my job as a producer in a TV newsroom. I witnessed first-hand the transformation occurring within the profession of journalism from the perspective of both avid consumer and professional producer. After a few years in the newsroom, my fascination with the matter and questions concerning its future far outweighed the answers. This book is a culmination of that passion, experience, and research. More importantly, it would not have happened without the help, support, and encouragement of many people along the way.

This book stems from my dissertation, which means it benefited from the invaluable guidance of my dissertation committee: Seth Lewis, Phil Napoli, Katya Ognyanova, and Matt Weber. I would especially like to thank Matt for the ongoing advice. It's impossible to overestimate his feedback on this book and all things academic. I would also like to express my gratitude to the many who have—whether they know it or not—provided invaluable inspiration and support throughout the development of this book through their own work, feedback, and encouragement: C. W. Anderson, Valerie Belair-Gagnon, Jan Lauren Boyles, Dan Kreiss, Jake Nelson, Cindy Royal, and Nikki Usher.

A very big thank you also goes to Andrew Chadwick for taking a chance on a first-time author and for his constructive, thoughtful, and encouraging feedback along the way. I am also thankful to my very patient editor, Angela Chnapko, and to the two anonymous reviewers who provided detailed and supportive feedback that truly helped turn this dissertation into a book.

I am grateful to Rutgers University and the Tow Center for Digital Journalism at Columbia University for their support throughout the early stages of data collection for this project. And, I am grateful to Fordham University, specifically the Gabelli School of Business, for supporting me throughout these final stages of the project. I am especially appreciative of the guidance and encouragement provided by Dean Donna Rapaccioli and the Communication and Media Management faculty, specifically Bozena Mierzejewska, Meghann Drury-Grogan, John Fortunato, John Carey, and Ronen Shay.

My biggest thanks goes to the Open News community and all the journalists who generously spent time with me for interviews, and without whom this book would certainly not exist. I am grateful for the thought-provoking conversations with Madi Alexander, Jeremy Bowers, Brian Boyer, Alvin Chang, Tyler Fisher, Brittany Mayes, Erin Medley, Elaine Piniat, Adam Playford, Rachel Schallom, CJ Sinner, Sarah Slobin, Sisi Wei, Ben Welsh, and Julia Wolfe. While others chose to remain anonymous, all deserve my deepest gratitude.

I am privileged to have had the opportunity to present parts of this book while in development at a number of conferences, which served to provide me with rich feedback as I tested the ideas. Some of the early material appears in Allie Kosterich and Matthew Weber (2019), Transformation of a modern newsroom workforce: A case study of NYC journalist network histories 2011–2015, *Journalism Practice*, 13, 431–457 and Allie Kosterich (2020), Managing news nerds: Strategizing about institutional change in the news industry, *Journal of Media Business Studies*, 17, 51–68.

Finally, I dedicate this book to my family, especially my husband Dan and our daughter Anna.

Introduction

News Nerds

Ben Welsh is the editor of the data and graphics department at the *Los Angeles Times*.

CJ Sinner is the digital graphics producer at the *Star Tribune*.

Alvin Chang is the senior data reporter at *The Guardian*.

Those are their titles, but are they journalists? The answer depends on whom you ask. More importantly, it depends on when you ask them. And then whatever the response may be, you must ask yourself why it matters at all.

Journalism, at the core, is the presentation of news through media. While the content of news has not changed much—headlines today are dominated by politicians, celebrities, wars, crime, and sports just as they were a century ago—how "journalists both gather and disseminate information has been turned on its head. Gone are the days of editors assigning stories to writers, who then research, inquire, and present what they found in a compelling yet accurate fashion.

"It had sort of a clerical assembly line attitude towards, well, here comes tomorrow's A-1 story, so let's slap a chart on it," Welsh, age 39, said. "It was part of that print newspaper factory, and that factory has closed. That assembly line is no longer needed."

As a modern journalist, Welsh's job is best explained through the narrative of his tenure at the *Los Angeles Times*. Around 2007, an opportunity arose to work at the *Los Angeles Times* website, which at the time, was still a separate web-only newsroom. The editor was looking for someone well versed in data and special projects while ready to focus those talents on digital journalism (i.e., stories for the web). And so began a digital special projects team at the *Los Angeles Times*, which merged the old computer-assisted reporting team with the web-projects team to focus on digital projects, data investigations, and news apps, and of which, Welsh eventually became the editor. For today's modern journalist and

News Nerds. Allie Kosterich, Oxford University Press. © Oxford University Press 2022.
DOI: 10.1093/oso/9780197500354.003.0001

for today's modern newsroom, this means, as Welsh explains, "gradually starting to catch up with reality:"

> It just feels dumb to say it, but the internet is not a fad. All of these digital projects and digital skills are not an accessory or like the third arm that somehow mutated off the body. They are the successor. They are the child in which we must invest and grow. That finally began to happen, literally just like two or three years ago. And so, the result is that our group, which was kind of happily and modestly successful in a small way in the corner of the newsroom, must gradually become more at the core of the newsroom, and part of the long, long, long overdue reform efforts.[1]

CJ Sinner explains a similar if not more personal transition and trajectory with regards to the profession of journalism:

> My first job in 2010 was an online producer in Bismarck, ND, and I sort of joke that they hired me because I was 22 and they were like, "oh this young person knows the internet." . . . And it became very clear, very quickly to me in that job, as an online producer, which I was pretty much the only digital person in that newsroom, how much more potential there was in online news that was not being tapped at least in that newsroom . . . I wanted to learn more code, and I also wound up getting quite a few data skills and video skills . . . I decided I still really have this love of data analysis and graphics, and so I really started to push my way more into that sphere to try and improve some of our print graphics online . . . Even after two years at the *Star Tribune*, it's not always clear to me what skills are needed or what the best use of my time is, and I think that's part of the challenge.[2]

Alvin Chang, who was the senior graphics reporter at Vox Media during the time of interviewing, describes a narrative that mirrors this transition from a "traditional" journalist (i.e., writing and reporting) to a profession stocked with a whole bag of technologically dependent and intricately intertwined journalistic skill sets from data and statistics to graphics and programming:

> In college, I was just a regular journalist wanting to work at like the *New Yorker*. I graduated in 2009 and that was the bottom of the recession. So instead of taking a metro reporter job at the *Daily News*, essentially, there was a job opening at ESPN as kind of an editor for the Insider section where they're using a lot of metrics and a lot of data

to do sports analytics. Being around all of that and not having the resources to necessarily travel to games or the time necessarily to do the reporting I needed to or the sources, I was left with a lot of data to kind of figure out how to add value to different stories. It started with me like copying and pasting a whole bunch of data to a website, to spreadsheets, and then like learning how to do the little things in Excel, and then slowly teaching myself how to do little bits of programming and eventually writing a whole bunch of data-driven pieces.

Chang moved on to the *Boston Globe* as a newsroom developer and data-visualization specialist, doing everything from programming to visual stories to data-driven investigative stories. The same mix of programming, data analysis, visualization, and design were all part of his next role at the *Connecticut Mirror* as well. "That was up until two years ago, and then I jumped to Vox," Chang explains. "I wanted a job where I would be working on my own stories, where I would be doing my own reporting, and both the reporting and output would be influenced by the technical skills I had or didn't have, but it would all be in service of journalism and the workflow of a reporter."[3]

Clearly, at some point over the last decade or so (2010–2020), the institutionalized, agreed-upon, and taken-for-granted perception of professional journalist took a turn. What the above narratives tell us is that the roles, responsibilities, and skill sets of today's journalist are fundamentally different than those of a traditional journalist. Welsh, Sinner, and Chang are news nerds—news industry professionals working in jobs at the intersection of traditional journalist positions and technologically intensive positions that were once largely separate. While the titles and specific responsibilities of news nerds vary, the commonality is a driving force to produce news more effectively and efficiently by harnessing the power of technological advancements such as the growth and accessibility of big data, computing technologies, networked devices, and mobile and social platforms. News nerds and their journalistic output reflect the increasing dependence of journalism on digital, technological developments. They are dependent on specific technological skills but remain in service of journalism and are incorporated into the workflow of the established journalist profession. Indeed, the institutionalized view of a professional journalist has changed. It has updated and augmented to account for news nerds. Understanding the reasons for that turn, its mechanics, timing, and impact are the goals of this book.

* * *

A 2009 headline in *New York Magazine* read, "What are these renegade cyber-geeks doing at The New York Times? Maybe saving it." The article focused on a team of developer-journalists, interactive producers, and visual editors tasked with creating experimental forms of storytelling. By capitalizing on developments in data, analytics, platform, and product capabilities, the team was able to create new forms of journalism, such as data-driven news applications and interactive graphics. The presence of cybergeeks in the newsroom, colloquially deemed "news nerds," serve as early indicators of change in the profession of journalism and call into question the core identity of who and what a journalist is today.

News nerds and the institutionalization of technical skills into the profession of journalism are the primary subjects of this book. It is thanks to ongoing technological development and associated societal changes that we find ourselves in an environment of constant transformation in which new types of skills, resources, processes, and organizations rapidly emerge and disappear. This context sets the stage for institutional change in which some new skills emerge and are institutionalized while others fail as fleeting fads, which creates a practical dilemma as organizations compete to attract the talent necessary to thrive and survive. In this book, my research brings to light the struggle of news organizations weighing the costs and benefits of investing in the hiring of news nerds; the struggle is contextualized in the broader forces of change that continue to impact the industry at large.

What makes this situation historically and practically interesting within the study of organizations, management, and journalism is that there was a time when the pervasive view of the profession was as an objective reporter, writer, and storyteller. Consider, as examples, the following definitions of journalism across the decades. In 1911, Walter Williams and Frank L. Martin wrote a book entitled *The Practice of Journalism, a Treatise on Newspaper Making*. In it, one working in the profession of journalism is characterized as being a "recorder, advocate, buyer and seller of news, judge, tribune, teacher, interpreter."[4] Qualifications of a journalist include "curiosity, the ability to look at facts and events fairly—from several points of view, the ability to work under pressure, to meet deadlines; honesty, fairness, objectivity; writing skills, including grammar and punctuation; typing skills; initiative—getting started and following through on a story; the ability to be at ease with different types of people; willingness to learn about all kinds of ideas, facts, people."[5]

A typical day in the life of a journalist might begin with an assignment from an editor, hours making phone calls to schedule appointments and interviews, and, of course, then going on site to conduct them. Writing would take up the bulk of the day, followed by a meeting with an editor who makes some suggestions for improvement. Once a story is completed, it is checked by a copy editor for grammar and spelling errors and then passed along to someone else for publishing.[6]

Contrast that to a day in the life of a news nerd, which as my fieldwork has shown, is anything but typical. News nerds are jacks- and jills-of-all-trades. They could arrive at their newsroom to fill in the company's homepage, read analytics, or train reporters on SEO (search engine optimization) headlines. Many times, they are working on creating graphics, visuals, or interactives through a mix of skills including reporting, design, data analysis, and programming. All of these tasks assumed while serving the core journalistic mission.

Indeed, at some point over the last decade or so (2010–2020), the institutionalized perception of the profession of journalism took a turn. Technology served the eviction notice. Developments in digital technologies increasingly shape the world around us, accelerating change at a rapid pace. The growing proliferation of data, coupled with advances in computational capabilities, facilitates tracking and analysis on an unforeseen scale.[7] Third-party platform companies on mobile devices increasingly mediate and deliver the news to consumers. Consumers are less likely to accept the traditional offerings that drove organizational success in the past.[8]

While many industries were disrupted—and continue to be disrupted—by these notions of automation and computation, few have changed as rapidly and publicly as the news industry.[9] This is, of course, compounded by the coronavirus pandemic, which like it did for many other sectors of the U.S. economy, has had a striking impact on the news industry. As a mirror into the impact on journalism, advertising revenue fell by a median of 42% year over year among the six publicly traded newspaper companies studied by the Pew Research Center.[10] These companies are major chains that own over 300 daily newspapers in the U.S. As Pew Research goes on to explain, ad revenue is historically the news industry's biggest revenue stream; while many newspapers have recently attempted to pivot their business models to subscription, overall circulation and subscription revenue has barely changed over the past decade.[11]

With drastic revenue decreases, news organizations moved to cut expenses—often in the form of payroll. Of the companies that reported compensation expenses in Pew's study, all showed double-digit percentage declines year over year. According to the Pew report, "this figure has been falling steadily over the past decade or more, reflecting the 51% decline in newspaper newsroom jobs between 2008 and 2019."[12]

Since 2011, total daily newspaper circulation has fallen by about 30% from 44.4 million to an estimated 28.6 million in 2018, and total revenue (advertising and audience) for U.S. newspapers has since decreased by about 25% from $37.1 million to an estimated $25.3 million in 2018.[13] There was a 9% decrease in newsroom employment—a loss of about 9,000 jobs—between 2008 and 2019.[14] Indeed, technological developments, coupled with associated economic realities and social changes, continue to disrupt the established practices of the profession of journalism and the news industry at large.

In the pages that follow, I explore how technological, economic, and societal changes are impacting journalism's hiring and training practices. I do so by drawing on a mixed-method research design combining interviews with professional journalists, textual analysis of trade press, and social network analysis of journalist career histories. Taken together, these data reveal the ways the institution of the profession of journalism is evolving to incorporate new technological skill sets and new routines of production.

In telling these stories and sharing these findings, I directly confront what happens when new skill sets and new ways of understanding and producing news start to collide with the old routines of journalism. What the case of journalism adds to our understanding of institutional change is the notion of an alternative outcome—institutional augmentation. In other words, the process of institutional change is not restricted to a binary outcome of reinstitutionalization of something new or failure as a fleeting fad; rather, there exists an alternative possibility in the updating and thus coexistence of supplementary institutions.

As journalism scholars Bernat Ivancsics and Mark Hansen write in a report on the future of the profession of journalism:

> We live in a data society. Journalists are becoming data analysts and data curators, and computation is an essential tool for reporting. Data and computation reshape the way a reporter sees the world and composes a story. They also control the operation of the information ecosystem she sends her journalism into, influencing where it finds audiences and generates discussion. So, every reporting beat is now a data beat, and computation is an essential tool for investigation.[15]

This is no more evident than with the coverage of the COVID-19 pandemic. The pandemic has impacted every facet of society, including the way that audiences consume news about it, as well as its impact on their lives. Interestingly, research conducted by YouGov suggests that audiences are demanding more data to understand COVID-19 and the vaccine; in fact, the majority of adults (73%) are specifically looking for facts and figures to help them understand the pandemic.[16] Indeed, as COVID-19 cases surged across the globe, so too did data visualizations, interactives, and investigative pieces. From the number of cases, the infection rate, the positivity rate, vaccinations administered, hospitalizations, and, horrifyingly, deaths, audiences have had to wrap their heads around more numbers and data at an exceedingly fast and potentially overwhelming pace. Maps, interactives, and data visualizations at large have become the go-to tools for communicating crucial and accessible information in everyday language.

And so, the work of news nerds paid off; even more so, news nerd work is critical to responding to current audience needs and maintaining the relevancy of journalism in today's society: seven out of ten people are more likely to trust news coverage on COVID-19 if it includes data to back it up.[17] The appetite and the need for news nerds and their work has never been greater; it's no surprise that news nerd output is at the forefront of coverage these days.

News nerds, such as those involved in the coverage of the COVID-19 pandemic, are indicative of the emergence of new forms of journalism and journalists that require new thinking. Any change in the agreed-upon understanding of who a journalist is impacts the production of news, news organization performance, and public perception, and thus necessitates attention to the particular role that these positions occupy within the profession of journalism, the news industry, and society at large.

Federica Cherubini, the head of Leadership Development at the Reuters Institute for the Study of Journalism explains the imperative to attending to news nerds as follows:

> These jobs are not easily categorized and are difficult to explain not only during a dinner party or in conversations with our parents—even colleagues battle to grasp their peculiarities . . . When you are creating a new role (and many of these are created by those who end up in them), it's difficult to know where you are going and what you're measuring yourself against. Newsrooms need to start thinking about establishing a real career path for their bridgers: What will happen when they leave? Will any one person be able to replace them, or are the roles too tailored to an individual? What kind of frameworks can be put in place?[18]

Indeed, the challenges facing news organizations today prompt critical questions about the complex dynamics surrounding institutional change in professions as a result of engagement with data, analytics, platform, and product technologies. According to news nerd Sisi Wei, who at the time of interviewing was the deputy editor of News Applications at ProPublica and is now the director of programs at OpenNews:

> Writing code, being able to understand data is integral to journalism as a whole. Journalists need to move in the same way that the world moves. Every industry is affected by big data right now, and if we can't understand it ourselves, we can't check what people are saying. The skills are accessible. Data journalism has been around for way longer than 2011, and one of the things that's so valuable is that we can check our sources. Oftentimes, we can correct people. That is so incredibly

helpful, especially for an industry where the main goal is to tell the truth. We need the tools to do so. (personal communication)

With the collision of new skill sets and new ways of understanding and producing news with the old routines of journalism, the findings of the case of news nerds have profound implications for the role of journalism in society by imploring us to think about processes necessary to sustain journalism and its ability to inform in contemporary society. With ongoing technological transformation, economic fluctuation, and changing social preferences comes the need for institutional augmentation in the profession of journalism and thus within news organizations themselves if they are to survive and thrive and continue (or, hopefully, improve) their role in informing society. As the case of news nerds illustrates, this imperative must be met with more than an emphasis on technology. It means strategic change throughout the whole of journalism through, for example, an emphasis on power structures; cultures of innovation and business literacy; career management for nontraditional skill sets; and diversity, equity, and inclusion as the news industry continues to grapple with the challenges of our digital society.

As such, the role of news organizations—and by extension, the profession of journalism—in the public sphere is increasingly more complex and proving more critical to society each day. Critical transformations have occurred in the ways that people consume news, for example, as seen in the development of social platforms and algorithmically tailored news feeds, tiny mobile screens, and the ability to bypass entire news organizations and instead access the public directly. The news industry, and particularly the case of news nerds, indeed serves as a window for furthering our understanding of how interactions among variances in professions are occurring in a new and significant way.

The Central Argument

The central argument of this book is that the profession of journalism has undergone institutional augmentation, an alternative to the process of institutional change that results in neither the displacement of an existing institution nor the failure of the new one. Instead, an existing institution (e.g., traditional journalists) is augmented, and in some ways, updated, to allow for the coexistence of a qualitatively and quantitatively distinct, supplementary institution (e.g., news nerds). To whit, news organizations increasingly integrate news nerds into the newsroom, and the relevance and legitimacy of news nerds is pervasive throughout the industry; however, news nerds are not fully diffused such that they work in every newsroom, nor have they displaced traditional journalists. In other words, not every traditional journalist is a news nerd; instead, the profession of journalism has undergone an update and augmented to allow for the space and coexistence of news nerds. This process of institutional augmentation has profound implications for news organizations, journalism, and society at large.

This overarching argument is explicated through several sub-arguments that correspond to the remaining chapters of the book. First, economic, technological, and social changes occurred outside the news industry that destabilized the established practices of the profession. One effect of these changes was the creation of an opportunity space for the emergence of new actors. Indeed, early stages of institutional augmentation in the profession of journalism were reflective of the entrance of outsiders from technology and science industries bringing new news nerd-related knowledge and expertise to the news industry. Interestingly, while early news nerd hires came from external industries, which may actually have accelerated the process of institutional change, current news nerd hires reinforce the existing practices of the news industry and the institutional influence of routines, and further support the idea of institutional augmentation and the coexistence of professional institutions without displacement or failure.

Second, change from within the industry occurred as organizations began to experiment and evaluate with new forms in the profession (i.e., news nerds). During the early stages of institutional change, organizations in legacy news sectors such as print news and broadcast news hired a greater number of news nerds compared to digital native news organizations. This pattern quickly reversed itself, shedding light on the importance of digital native news organizations as leaders in the hiring of news nerds, which further reflects the flexibility and adaptability to change of these newer entrants.

Third, news nerds as an institutionalized form of professional journalist require legitimacy. Broadly, this need is met through three mechanisms. Morally, legitimacy of news nerds occurs via normative alignment, such as through the creation of news nerd related journalism education programs. Pragmatically, legitimacy of news nerds is evident through the acknowledgment of the relationship between news nerd production output and financial benefits to news organizations. Cognitive legitimacy of news nerds is represented in the achievements of news nerds through their day-to-day work and recognition of that work with prestigious awards and other formal honors.

Fourth, the community of news nerds both within news organizations and across the news industry continues to grow and diffuse as news nerds gain prominence within the profession. News nerds are often justified as a potential solution to the specified challenges associated with constant change, and their community is increasingly visible in the form of professional organizations and conferences. The growing number of newsrooms with news nerd teams and the rising number of job listings hiring for news nerd positions provides evidence for continued diffusion.

Lastly, institutional augmentation in the profession of journalism and this collision of old routines of journalism with news ways of understanding and doing newswork implores us to think about organizational processes necessary to sustain the profession and the news industry at large. In the case of news nerds, this means more than emphasis on the latest technology. It means strategic change throughout the whole of news organizations through an emphasis on power structures; cultures of innovation and business literacy; career management for nontraditional skill sets; and diversity, equity, and inclusion as the news industry continues to grapple with the challenges of our digital society.

Together, these arguments fit within the institutional perspective on change in professions that has long focused on how professions—and industry-wide structures more generally—become routines that are taken for granted.[19] This view provides a foundation for examining the relationship between external social, political, economic, and technological forces and organizational structures, such as professions.[20] Historically, scholarship heeds that professions control their own fate[21] and determine their own definition and purview; however, recent and rapid technological and associated social change has increased the influence of external forces.

Outline of the Book

This book tells the story of institutional change in the profession of journalism, specifically in its augmentation to allow for the emergence, establishment, and coexistence of news nerds. It does so according to an analytical framework of institutional augmentation, and thus, does not always match up chronologically. Instead, the focus is on the various factors necessary for the process to occur, and so, the book is organized accordingly.

Chapter 1 details and explicates an analytical framework for understanding who news nerds are, how they emerged and evolved within the broader field of professional journalism, and why it matters that they did. Building on the rich scholarship in journalism studies, I discuss the boundaries and central tenets of professional journalists and review recent changes throughout the news industry, including an explication of the development of news nerds. I then outline the theoretical argument for analyzing institutional change in a profession and argue its relevance for the case of professional journalists. The chapter closes with an abridged discussion of the research context and methods (see the Appendix for further details on the data and methods used to support the argument of this book).

Chapter 2 considers the technological, economic, and social events that contributed to the destabilization of the established news industry practices. Drawing on analysis of interviews with industry practitioners and a large body of industry documents, the evidence suggests that these changes created an opportunity space for the entrance of new players outside the traditional boundaries of the news industry. These new entrants came in the form of emergent actors and organizations bringing in new skills and expertise that led to further deinstitutionalization of the profession. The chapter then turns to a case study of journalist employment networks, which shows that early news nerd hires came from industries external to news such as technology and marketing; however, as the institutional change process progressed, news nerd hires were increasingly driven from within the news industry itself.

Chapter 3 charts the beginning of extant news organizations' experimentation with and evaluation of news nerds. Drawing again on analysis of both interviews and industry documents, Chapter 3 focuses primarily on changes from within the industry. Here again, I turn to the case study of journalist employment networks, which helps shed light on several of these patterns through social network analysis. The case study specifically allows for comparisons between legacy news organizations and new entrants (e.g., at the time, digital native news organizations) and capitalizes on the differences between their hiring practices of news nerds to better understand the role of factors such as extant organizational experimentation in institutional change over time.

Chapter 4 examines the role of legitimacy in the institutional augmentation of journalists for news nerds. Analysis of interviews and industry documents suggests that news nerd legitimacy is manifested in three ways: as moral legitimacy through, for example, the increasing emphasis on news nerd skills at journalism schools; as pragmatic legitimacy through the increasing connection between news nerd output and audience engagement and business returns; and as cognitive legitimacy, through the increase in media coverage of news nerds and the awards won by their work. Regression analyses of journalist employment data provide systematic assessments of the relationship between legitimacy and news nerds at both the professional and organizational levels.

Chapter 5 traces the overall objectification and justification of news nerds as a solution to the ongoing challenges faced by the news industry. Furthermore, in addition to the analysis of interviews and industry documents, an examination of this last institutional change factor provides a supplementary data source. In receiving access to an exclusive data set of journalism industry job listings, I am able to quantitatively and qualitatively provide evidence of the growing diffusion of news nerds throughout the news industry over time. Here again, the case study of journalist employment networks further complements these findings by demonstrating how the diffusion patterns are enacted at the organizational and professional levels.

The final chapter reviews the argument in an integrated fashion and then explores the implications of institutional augmentation and news nerds. The collision of old and new as depicted through the institutional augmentation of the journalism profession for news nerds implores us to rethink how journalism continues to survive, as well as ideally thrive, in its role of informing society. Indeed, this means more than an emphasis on technology. First, as the case of news nerds shows us, journalism requires strategic change throughout the profession by disentangling and revamping power structures and career paths to emphasize access to data, code, and a general culture of experimentation. Second, journalism of the future must foster cultures of innovation and business literacy with an openness to new approaches and business models. And finally, the case of news nerds illustrates that for journalism to survive, it must find new ways to meet audience needs and new ways to represent the audience it serves.

In examining the intersection of institutional change and the journalist profession, it is my hope that this book contributes to three major conversations by (1) mapping the growth of news nerds within the broader news industry; (2) introducing the notion of institutional augmentation as a solution to the extant binary options for institutional change outcomes; and (3) investigating the implications of institutional augmentation and specifically of news nerds for both industry and society at large.

While the phenomenon analyzed in this book is specific to the context of journalism, it is, of course, relevant for industries other than news (e.g., cultural industries such as music). This book builds on the premise that modern society is inherently digital and data centric, and building on that premise it unpacks the mechanisms of change both internal and external to the news industry that gave rise to the emergence and growth of news nerds. In doing so, this book theoretically teases apart the difference between when something new is real and substantial—as in, an institution—as opposed to when it is a trend—as in, a failed fad, or when something new cannot simply be classified based on a binary choice—as in the case of news nerds.

1

Institutional Change and the Profession of Journalism

There are ways in which they're different from journalists writ large . . . There's a whole other domain of skills which are often summarized as computer programming but also includes things like information design, visual storytelling techniques, and a kind of innovative attitude to finding new ways to tell stories. They include a problem-solving mindset around technology and storytelling forums that is beyond reading Roy Peter Clark's six ways to write a news story . . . There has been all this effort throughout the years—that was well meaning—to like help people write in these different techniques. But there's a whole other set of techniques that you need to tell stories with these other forms—learning those forms, helping to develop new versions of those forms, being comfortable with the uncertainty of how to navigate a marketplace where tall of these forms are emerging . . . To me, it is computer programming, it is data, it is using data as a raw material to tell stories, and it is using different techniques to communicate than a traditional written story.[1]

The above quote from news nerd Ben Welsh, editor of the Data and Graphics Department at the *Los Angeles Times*, describes the acute differences between news nerds and the more traditional view of a journalist, or the profession of journalism at large. In essence, the common force driving news nerds is to produce more effective and efficient news by harnessing the power of technological advancements. As an augmentation of the profession of journalism, news nerds and their journalistic output reflect the increasing dependence of newswork on digital technological skill sets while remaining in service of the established tenets of journalism.

Prior to answering how news nerds became an augmentation in journalism, we first need to discuss the historical and theoretical underpinnings of the profession of journalism. The term "professional journalist" is used throughout this

News Nerds. Allie Kosterich, Oxford University Press. © Oxford University Press 2022.
DOI: 10.1093/oso/9780197500354.003.0002

book to refer to those workers agreed upon by both fellow practitioners and the public as having the particular talent, knowledge, and education to fulfill the key role of creating editorial projects for public consumption and in the public interest.[2] Professions are sustained with taken-for-granted norms regarding "who does what, under what circumstances."[3] Any change in the agreed upon understanding of journalism profession can thus impact the production of news, as well as news organizational performance, and public perception of news industry. Given this influence, professional journalists play a significant role within the news industry and society at large.

While the specific attributes that make up the notion of a professional journalist vary, there is considerable agreement surrounding a few general dimensions including the application of a mastery of skills and a body of knowledge to the work, which is self-regulated due to distinctive codes and ethics, and autonomous and prestigious as compared to others.[4] The news industry maintains certain agreed-upon expectations regarding the definition of the journalism profession and they create an ideology that serves to continuously reinforce that consensus. At its fundamental core, the professional journalist has control over content, deciding and defining what the public sees about the world.[5]

Traditionally, there is no sanctioned body of knowledge that defines the profession; however, core skills such as reporting and writing are identifiable. Introductory textbooks typically define a journalist as someone who reports and writes accurate information for dissemination to a wider audience. While the U.S. news industry does not have a regulatory entrance exam, as is the case in many other professions, professional journalists share a broad code of conduct, standards of practice, and ethical guidelines that focus on the imperative to serve the public interest. This includes dominant journalistic structures such as the *AP Stylebook*, professional associations (e.g., the Society of Professional Journalists and Online News Association), and accrediting agencies such as the Accrediting Council on Education in Journalism and Mass Communication.

Unfortunately, "agreed-upon expectations" are oftentimes insufficient for maintaining an impenetrable understanding of a profession. Lacking a sanctioned body of knowledge, professional journalists struggle to maintain exclusivity.[6] Professional journalists are sometimes categorized as those skilled in information gathering, other times as those skilled in information presentation, and even sometimes as those skilled in a combination of both, in addition to audience interaction.[7] The guiding principle behind the profession of journalism is often reduced to the importance of unbiased and fact-based reporting, and even that authority is currently contested.[8]

As such, there is no dearth of recent scholarship on the changing definition of professional journalist.[9] The boundaries were perhaps simpler in the past and grounded in a professional ideology and code of ethics. In recent years, however, emergent actors have entered the industry, increasingly blurring these lines.

News Nerds

Exclusivity challenges in the journalism profession combined with advancements in the technologies used to produce news have contributed to recent change, including the emergence of new actors and new forms of professional journalists. Interestingly, there is a great deal of work on the tensions between new and existing forms of newswork as it is well established that professional journalists have long used new forms of technology to accomplish their work.[10] When photojournalists joined the newsroom in the 1930s with the adoption of wire photos, for example, they too were met with resistance as a new form of professional expertise.[11] Later, however, when visual journalists joined the newsroom, their routines aligned more closely with those of traditional journalists and less conflict ensued.[12]

Together, these instances support the notion that technological development often serves as a stimulus for the possibility of new professional forms. Journalism scholars Seth Lewis and Oscar Westlund interrogate this relationship between technology and journalism by introducing a spectrum of the dependence of various forms of newswork on various forms of technology including four classifications from human-centric journalism to technology-supported journalism to technology-infused journalism to technology-oriented journalism.[13] This spectrum helps shed light on the wide range of newswork activities and their varying dependence on technological actants.

In addition to new technologies, however, new forms of professional journalists are also connected to changing social conditions such as the increasing demand for mobile and social content, as well as changing market conditions such as the increasing financial challenges and competition. In one assessment, C. W. Anderson, Emily Bell, and Clay Shirky declared that the news industry is no longer predictable; uniform editorial processes, revenues, and professional identities are elements of a past profession. "The extent to which a journalist now needs to have in-depth knowledge about something other than journalism is increasing"; in addition to storytelling skills, modern professional journalists require data literacy, an understanding of metrics and audiences, and coding capabilities.[14] What Anderson et al. point to is an issue that others in management have observed across domains—random technological change, along with the unpredictable nature of industry, is a key driver of long-term change.[15] In the context of journalism, the classic view of a professional journalist as an objective reporter, writer, and storyteller no longer stands as the singular paradigm for the profession at large.

An alternative to the taken-for-granted understanding of the profession of journalism is developing as news organizations increasingly realize that moving stories beyond words is a critical component for newsrooms everywhere, that understanding and working with data is a prized skill, and that being able to tell stories that resonate socially is a crucial component of a successful business model. Take, for example, the rise of interactive journalism and the journalists who produce it through a combination of software programming and storytelling skills. Journalism scholar Nikki Usher offers a deep-dive account into the development of this specific subspecialty by arguing that the broader economic, technological, and social environment within which journalism operates created the conditions for interactive journalism to emerge. Usher defines interactive journalism as the "visual presentation of storytelling through code for multilayered, tactile user control for the purpose of news and information."[16] Other scholars have noted similar patterns in the rise of programmer-journalists[17] and news application developers,[18] roles that bridge the gap between engineering and journalists.

The rise of interactive journalism and news applications is intricately intertwined with data journalism,[19] which is "gathering, cleaning, organizing, analyzing, visualizing, and publishing data to support the creation of acts of journalism."[20] In their book on the regeneration of news, journalism scholars Alfred Hermida and Mary Lynn Young illustrate how the emergence and continual rise of data journalism as a subspecialty of the profession is a response to the effects of digital disruption.[21] In applying computation and data science to journalism, data journalism too blends the cultures of technology and journalism.

There is also an increasing presence of journalists focused on social media content and analytics of audience behavior data, which is utilized both to better calibrate newsgathering activities[22] and even to produce news.[23] As journalism scholar Nicole Blanchett Neheli describes, these digital editors "sit cemented to monitors, working to decipher what stories have or are gaining traction. Using this information, they choose placement of content, enhance stories, and share stories via social media to build traffic."[24] As a whole, these social media editors, engagement editors, and growth editors bring audience analytics into the newsroom and lead growth initiatives within an editorial mindset.

New technologies and changing social conditions have indeed created an opportunity space for new forms of journalism to emerge that are interactive, visual, data driven, and/or uniquely linked to audience engagement. As journalism scholars Brian Creech and Andrew Mendelson explain, "At the center of these changes often rests an idealized notion of the technologically adept journalist who creates compelling content by mastering digitally based techniques of reporting, producing, and distributing the news."[25] Each of these developments challenges the traditional expectations of what journalists know how to do.

Taken together, these developments signal the emergence of new forms of newswork and change in the profession and further indicate a new "wave" of journalism transformation.[26] This wave reflects transformation beyond the transition from print to digital and toward a focus on professional journalists working at the intersection of news and data, analytics, mobile and social platforms, and/or products. It builds from this collection of emerging scholarship and anecdotal evidence of the growth in alternatives to the taken-for-granted understandings and expectations of the profession of journalism to support the premise that there is a concerted increase in the prominence of news nerds throughout the industry.

News nerds hold a variety of job positions throughout the news industry, ranging from data editor to audience development editor to news applications editor. The common thread behind each of these positions is a driving force to produce more effective and efficient news by harnessing the power of technological advancements such as the rise and accessibility of big data, computing technologies, networked devices, and mobile platforms. Harkening back to the scholarship of Lewis and Westlund and the spectrum of journalism's dependence on technology, news nerds can be viewed as technology-infused journalists: journalists "institutionalizing technology for production and distribution—and, as a result, becoming increasingly dependent on technological actants even as they become empowered by them."[27] In other words, the work of news nerds is not simply supported or augmented by technological developments but also dependent on and intricately intertwined with them.

Responsibilities of news nerds take the form of activities such as building tools, creating graphics, making interactive story templates, or analyzing large data sets. Skills range from web development, to coding and programming, to data analytics and visualization. Importantly, news nerds are reporters, journalists, and editors—proficient in writing and news judgment, and working in the name of producing better stories and making sure they get to and engage with the right audiences.

The output of news nerds also varies, ranging from traditional text or visual stories driven by investigation of large data sets, to tailored editorial production and distribution priorities grounded in audience analytics, to interactive graphics or news applications created via web development or programming. For example, in 2015, the *Tampa Bay Times*' ran an award-winning investigative series called "Failure Factories" that traced the decline of schools in St. Petersburg's black neighborhoods. The series, which appeared both online and in print, was driven by analysis of a large-scale data set from the Florida Department of Education.[28] Another example of news nerd work is *The Wall Street Journal*'s social media coverage of the killing of two WDBJ journalists on live TV, which was fueled by real-time audience analytics.[29] News nerd work also includes interactive features such as, and perhaps most famously, "Snow Fall: The Avalanche at Tunnel Creek" by *The New York Times*, which integrated text, photos, videos, graphics, animations, maps, and code to create a stand-alone news application.[30] More recently, news nerd work is increasingly pervasive. See, for example, how quickly major news organizations turned out stand-alone coronavirus products such as *The New York Times'* interactive product tracking global virus and vaccine development[31] or ProPublica's multitude of coronavirus news apps.[32]

News nerds and their work are dependent on specific technical skills but remain in the service of journalism and incorporated into the workflow of the established profession of journalism. It is thus important to clarify that the study of news nerds is not about the technological developments per se, but reflective of the way that technology impacts the job of professional journalists. Furthermore, not all of these positions are fundamentally *new*. Data journalism, for example, grew out of computer-assisted reporting (CAR) beginning in the 1950s.[33] While a detailed history is outside the scope of this book, there are several excellent studies on the history of CAR, data journalism, and web developers in news.[34]

Instead, the goal here is to understand the path of change—grounded in technological advancement and development but enacted in the name of news and storytelling—in the prescribed positions of professional journalists that were not possible in the past. The notion that there is now a journalist in the newsroom responsible for remixing and interpreting data, and then presenting a narrative around it through an interactive framework is qualitatively different than the CAR journalist and separate web developers in news organizations of the past. Indeed, there is no denying that the emergence and growth of news nerds provide a fruitful context in which to investigate the dynamics of institutional change in a profession.

In sum, news nerds represent the merging of data, analytic, and platform responsibilities and expertise with journalistic storytelling that were once generally separate. By this, I am not arguing that basic understandings of news are changing nor trying to overstate the existence of news nerds. Instead, I mean that the notion of who is a journalist (and who can be one) is augmenting. News nerds include those who practice data-driven investigative reporting and interactive platform storytelling as well as those who use analytics to bring in new readers and deliver information. News nerds are not simply journalists supported by technological developments but are also intricately intertwined with them so far as they are institutionalized for production and distribution. It is an important distinction to understand and one worthy of investigation. In the past, news nerds were two separate departments in a news organization and thus they currently defy traditional professional categorization and boundaries. Hence, news nerds are augmenting the traditionally institutionalized space of journalists versus technology workers (in a news organization), highlighting that one of the core contributions of this work is that it suggests a space between change and continuity, or, in other words, institutional augmentation.

Institutional Change

The core question at this point is how news nerds became an institutionalized augmentation of the profession of journalism. Depending on the theoretical perspective, there are a number of possible avenues for examining how structures—for instance, an industry's professions, policies, or practices—emerge and evolve with regard to the external environment. From a strategic management perspective, on the one hand, professions are structures that are strategically adapted responses to uncertain external elements.[35] Similarly, resource dependency theory (RDT) is premised on the notion that organizations require external resources for survival, which are influenced by an organization's ability to manage dependencies on other organizations.[36] In general, these theories both largely assume organizations are agency-laden actors responsible for boundedly rational adaption to external circumstances.

An institutional approach, on the other hand, conceptualizes change as the result of interaction among broader external forces and highlights the role of the routinized rules and ideas that engender organizations. Institutional theory has a long-standing focus on how practices become routinized and taken for granted.[37] Institutional theorist Scott explains that "institutions consist of cognitive, normative, and regulative structures and activities that provide stability and meaning to social behavior. Institutions are transported by various carriers—culture, structures, and routines—and they operate at multiple levels of jurisdiction."[38] Thus, an institutional approach to change provides a foundation for examining the relationship between broader social, political, economic, and technological forces and taken-for-granted structures such as a profession.

Early institutional studies portrayed efficient change as a challenge due to the necessity of compliance with various institutional structures; as such, this compliance was oftentimes symbolic and decoupled from an organization's core technical activities.[39] In other words, change might be communicated or executed in an ad hoc manner but was not thoroughly integrated into an organization's core business model, processes, and functions. Powell and DiMaggio expand on that foundational premise by explicating the role of institutional rules in legitimizing organizational structures.[40] Indeed, an institutional approach attends to the ways that external forces impact organizational action by providing meaning through regulative, normative, and cognitive systems.

While the foundational scholarship tended to focus on persistence, stability, and compliance throughout an industry,[41] more recent scholarship turned toward a broad focus on understanding how institutional structures change.[42] Of specific interest were topics such as who or what initiates institutional change,[43] resistance to change,[44] and the impact of change.[45] Indeed, an institutional approach is often applied to further understanding of the ways that new structures (e.g., professions, policies, practices) diffuse throughout an industry to become a taken-for-granted routine.

There is a long history of institutional approaches to the study of the news industry. While much of this work traditionally focuses on news as an institution in and of itself,[46] scholars have recently started using an institutional approach to examine how external social, technological, economic, and political forces institutionally shape structures within the industry. Journalism scholar Lowrey, for example, found that news organizations tend to reinforce institutional norms while struggling to innovate during uncertain times; specifically, organizations were decoupling internal production processes from external manifestations of industry trend adoption.[47] This is a practical instantiation of Meyer and Rowan's earlier explicated tenet—changes, trends would be communicated or even adopted in an ad hoc manner, but news organizations struggled to actually integrate them into their core production processes. Other studies—if not explicitly, then at least implicitly—also reflect institutional tendencies of news organizations. Isomorphism, for example, is evident throughout the industry as the imitation found in news organizations' adoption of technological innovations.[48]

Furthermore, incumbent resistance is reflected in the continued support of the status quo as legacy news organizations struggle to incorporate new digital processes into news production.[49] Journalism scholar Boczkowski examined legacy news organizations shifting to digital production and highlighted the ways organizational and professional dynamics challenge the news industry's relationship with change.[50] Similarly, Ryfe concluded that journalists in a case study of three newsrooms did not adapt well to innovation because of their strong institutionalized norms, which often conflicted with change.[51]

With this book, I build from earlier scholarship to consider institutional change in journalism as a profession comprised of interconnected actors, technologies, audiences, and activities and subject to similar institutional pressures.[52] In doing so, I strive to "account for the people who actually do the work."[53] As such, this book heeds recent calls in journalism scholarship to interrogate transformation within the wider context of changes in work and employment.[54]

INSTITUTIONAL CHANGE IN PROFESSIONS

An institutional approach to professions offers a framework that accounts for change in an industry's taken-for-granted understanding of its workers—the people who actually do the work. A profession is comprised of those occupational incumbents for whom control over a task relates to explicit knowledge from training.[55] The primary duties of a profession are only realized by those with a particular talent, knowledge, or education.[56]

Professions hold an important role in society and, historically, professions were stable and in control of their own purview.[57] Recent scholarship, however, has attended to the influence of external pressures on the work of professions.[58] As one example of an institutional structure, professions represent a mechanism for ordering, creating, and providing meaning to a distinct area of organizational life.[59]

It follows, then, that professions are institutionally shaped by a variety of forces that can change from a combination of new people, places, and technologies, which would thus push professions into new and unexamined area. In other words, change influences the construction of professions as organizations strive to communicate alignment with institutional norms and practices.[60] Any change in a profession thus impacts the taken-for-granted understanding about who does what and when, and so attention must be directed at the process of institutional change in professions.

Indeed, the relationship between professions and institutional change is an intimately intertwined path. Institutional change in professions, specifically within the context of the external environment within which work takes place, can occur along three different dimensions: content and procedures; terms and contracts (e.g., pay and hours); and conditions, which include changes in staffing and resources.[61] A growing body of work applies an institutional change perspective to the study of professions that highlights the importance of a profession's dependence on broader institutional patterns and norms,[62] as well as the interconnectedness of professional, organizational, and institutional transformation.[63]

The Process of Institutional Augmentation

With the aforementioned institutional approach in mind, one may begin to interrogate the emergence and establishment of news nerds. Prior institutional scholarship provides a starting point for explaining the process, or what Greenwood et al. would call the six stages of institutional change: precipitating jolts, deinstitutionalization, preinstitutionalization, theorization, diffusion, and reinstitutionalization.[64] According to this model, institutionalization begins when social, technological, or regulatory jolts disrupt and destabilize established structures, which provides an opportunity space for the emergence of new actors to introduce new ideas. Experimentation with new ideas and eventual formalization of new arrangements in organizational policies enhances moral and pragmatic legitimacy. Something new becomes fully legitimate as it is increasingly adopted and diffused throughout an industry until finally, it is reinstitutionalized as the taken-for-granted and appropriate option—displacing the original—or it is ultimately rejected. In synthesizing the literature and applying this model to the case of the journalism profession, I propose, instead, a framework of institutional augmentation based on four main factors: (1) precipitating jolts and deinstitutionalization, (2) experimentation and evaluation, (3) legitimization, and (4) diffusion.

PRECIPITATING JOLTS AND DEINSTITUTIONALIZATION

Precipitating jolts in the external environment such as social, technological, or regulatory triggers disrupt stabilized practices of an industry.[65] Early studies of institutional change focused on exogenous jolts occurring at the societal level such as technological developments, regulatory changes, and social upheaval, and the effect these jolts have on established industries in triggering institutional change industries. Other research on the precipitating triggers of institutional change includes a more agentic focus on institutional entrepreneurs—agents of change with an interest in particular institutional structures and the resources to change them[66] and a practice-oriented focus on change driven by worker activities.[67] In sum, this research supports the notion that precipitating jolts create uncertain and tense conditions that thus stimulate institutional change.

Uncertainty, in other words, creates an opportunity for deinstitutionalization, which is characterized by the emergence of new entrants introducing new ideas, possibilities, and efforts at change.[68] Research on deinstitutionalization is often focused on initiators of institutional change and those coming from outside the traditional boundaries on an industry. As peripheral players, these new entrants are more adept at developing ideas of change since they are less likely to be connected to established players and therefore less constrained by institutional norms and practices.[69] Oftentimes, new entrants initiate change because they are disadvantaged by existing institutional arrangements;[70] however, in other circumstances, they are identified as those with the resources or ability to solve specified problems in an industry.[71]

In the case of the profession of journalism, precipitating jolts are exemplified through technological developments such as the growing ubiquity of the internet, advances in data and computational capabilities, and mobile and social

platforms. These technological developments are coupled with associated economic realities and social changes of the past decade that continue to disrupt
the established practices of the news industry and challenge what it means to
be a professional journalist. Economic realities (e.g., the Great Recession and a
general decrease in news organizations' revenues) are indeed crucial to the rise
of news nerds who promise to make news more efficiently and effectively. In a
time when managers are in desperate search for profitable business models, the
opportunity for some individuals to do new things in journalism serves as an
attractive innovation. Indeed, many of the changes that undermined established
industry practices also served as disruptive shocks that created an opportunity
space for alternative approaches and the emergence of new players from outside
the traditional boundaries of news. New entrants in the form of tech-centered
digitally native news organizations (at the organizational level) and software programmers (at the actor level) offered an alternative approach to the established
practices and processes of the profession, igniting the possibility of change and
thus representing deinstitutionalization.

EXPERIMENTATION AND EVALUATION

The second factor necessary for institutional augmentation is experimentation
and evaluation, which occurs when a few organizations independently begin
to adopt a new structure in an ad hoc manner. Organizations independently
monitor competitor efforts, assessing the risk of implementing/adopting a new
structure.[72] At this point, there are very few adopters of a new institutional structure, and the extent of implementation varies considerably, but it represents the
beginning of establishment and formalization of something new.

   In response to the challenges associated with meeting the needs of technological and social disruption and producing more innovative, accessible, and engaging content, an alternative to the profession of journalism emerged in the form
of news nerds. Experimentation and shifts in organizational structures dedicated
to exploring the potential of news nerds were representative of this stage, reflecting an attempt by legacy news organizations to understand and engage with the
new playing field. Experimentation and evaluation of news nerds at this point,
however, was conducted on an ad hoc basis and not fully integrated into newsroom routines or business models.

LEGITIMIZATION

While destabilization and experimentation are common to a wide range of
change processes, the third factor identified—legitimization—is specific to
institutional change.[73] Legitimacy is the socially constructed general perception

of appropriateness and taken-for-granted understanding of reality that plays an essential role in institutional change.[74] Legitimacy can take a variety of forms depending on the context and the audience; in general, it can be synthesized as a perception, a judgment, or the consequences of perception and judgment as "manifested in actors' action" such as acceptance or endorsement.[75] Organizational scholar Mark Suchman provides a breakdown of typologies that includes moral legitimacy (normative approval), pragmatic legitimacy (self-interest), and cognitive legitimacy (comprehensibility and taken-for-grantedness).[76]

Moral legitimacy, for one, is the "nesting of new ideas within prevailing normative prescriptions."[77] The moral legitimacy of something new is evident when it is integrated into industry norms such as training and policies. Here, the premise is based on the recognition that skill, effort, and practice are each also necessary conditions for legitimacy.[78] This is evident in the increasingly common connection between news nerds and associated skills, training, and expertise provided at the professional training grounds of journalism school.

Pragmatic legitimacy, on the other hand, is grounded in self-interest and functional superiority.[79] This type of legitimacy involves the linking of something new with actual economic outcomes.[80] The pragmatic legitimacy of news nerds is established via the relationship with their output and audience traffic, engagement, and business returns.

Lastly, cognitive legitimacy involves an increase in public knowledge and awareness and acceptance of a new idea by external stakeholders.[81] A central tenet of this type of legitimacy is the idea that legitimacy is located within the audience as a shared and taken-for-granted perception.[82] As such, cognitive legitimacy is generally understood through the observations and assessments of those external to an industry's profession such as through the increase in media coverage of news nerds or the prestigious awards won by their work, which can shape the configuration of a profession and thus impact institutional change.

DIFFUSION

Legitimization is followed by diffusion,[83] during which something new is adopted until it reaches the final stage of institutional change and is recognized as appropriate by the proper actors within an industry.[84] Indeed, diffusion only occurs if new ideas are objectified as an increasingly visible alternative and compellingly justified as the solution to a specified problem.[85] In other words, the adoption of something new by a few others indicates a level of effectiveness that increases legitimacy and encourages wider adoption and diffusion.[86] This occurs as organizations engage in isomorphic behavior, modeling themselves after others that are perceived as legitimate and thus developing common exchange patterns.[87]

Throughout the news industry, the hiring of news nerds is often justified as a potential solution to the specified challenges associated with technological, economic, and social change. Objectification is established via the increasingly visible community of news nerds in the form of professional organizations and conferences. Furthermore, demand continues to follow suit as evident in the growing number of newsrooms with news nerd teams and the rising number of job listings hiring for news nerd positions.

INSTITUTIONAL AUGMENTATION

Elements of the four-pronged framework outlined earlier can be found in previous case studies on institutional change; however, in almost all instances, scholarship heeds that the final stage of institutional change is a binary option, occurring when something new is either reinstitutionalized as the taken-for-granted "natural and appropriate arrangement" or ultimately rejected as a fleeting fad.[88] In response and in studying the profession of journalism, I present the above framework of *institutional augmentation,* and I argue that it can help explain the case of news nerds and change processes in a wide range of industries that result in stable diffusion without full institutionalization—an outcome that differs from the traditional binary options of reinstitutionalization or failure.

To illustrate, the reinstitutionalization of news nerds would mean that there is no longer a distinction to be made between them and traditional journalists. At the most basic level, reinstitutionalization could be reflected with an elimination of the qualification from journalist job titles. In other words, a data editor would not be different from an interactives editor or a news editor—they would all just be editors using any tools necessary to tell the best stories and get them in front of the right audiences. For some on the inside of the news industry, this has always been the case. As one news nerd explained to me:

> There is no distinction for me. I know what stories to tell and [which] will be great for journalism and those stories require certain skill sets, and I use them to tell the stories that I want to tell ... [The news industry] needs to move away from focusing on the technology and focus instead on the content.[89]

Clearly, however, that lack of distinction is not the current status throughout the profession at large. News nerds are not so generalizable that there is no longer any differentiation between them and traditional journalists. In other words, news nerds have not been reinstitutionalized, however, nor have they failed as a trend or fad. Furthermore, this status is expected to endure over time. It is not expected that in a few decades, every professional journalist will be a news nerd nor will the notion of news nerds have fizzled out.

I expect that the current institutional status of the profession of journalism will not be displaced. Practically, it is reasonable to predict that news nerds serve (and will continue to serve) as an augmentation of the profession as illustrated with the following quote, which highlights the non-reciprocal relationship between traditional journalists and news nerds:

> I learned how to write code on the job at one point, and now I basically could be a computer software engineer at a computer software engineering company. Why couldn't someone do that while they were also working at a newspaper? I don't really see any reason why that's not something someone could do. I don't think it's something that everyone should do—right, it takes a lot of time, it takes a lot of effort, you have to put a lot of energy into it to be good at it, and there are people here who are using 150 percent of their energy to ask the president hard questions. Should they be also learning to write code? No. They should be working with other people who are good at that and communicating what they need in a way that it can get done.[90]

In other words, any journalist can be a news nerd with the right training, but not every journalist should be a news nerd—they are not interchangeable, they are not one and the same. Instead, the profession of journalism has augmented enough so that both can coexist without one displacing the other.

Of course, the process of institutional change in the context of the profession of journalism continues to unfold. While it is reasonable to expect that institutional augmentation will hold for some time to come, the future of news nerds cannot be predicted or guaranteed. Questions remain as to whether news nerds will be an accepted, stable, and unquestioned professional structure in every newsroom. The aim of the book, however, is to explain news nerds, and the institutional augmentation framework serves to organize the forces at play so we can understand who they are, how they came to be, and why it matters.

Research Context: U.S. News Industry 2011–2020

This book offers a recent history of the modern profession of journalism and a decade-long analysis of news nerds from 2011 to 2020. Here, I argue that news nerds are in large part an institutional augmentation of the profession of journalism—qualitatively and quantitatively distinct yet coexisting as taken-for-granted forms in the profession of journalism. The emergence and current institutional status of news nerds is driven by four main factors: disruptive forces destabilizing the established practices of the news industry and allowing the entrance of new players; experimentation with and evaluation of new forms of the journalist profession; legitimization; and eventual diffusion of news nerds throughout the industry.

To explain the rise of news nerds, what makes one, and the implications of their existence, I draw on evidence from the ten-year period of 2011 to 2020. The focus is on the most recent "wave" of journalism transformation[91]—past the shift of print news organizations to the web and the emergence of digital native news—and toward the rise of data, analytics, social and mobile platforms, and products. Indeed, the 2010s have been assessed as a "critical"[92] and "constitutive"[93] moment for journalism as the profession grapples with new positions and skill sets resulting from ongoing technological and economic disruption, as well as associated changes in news production and consumption.

As is more thoroughly explicated in the Data and Methods Appendix, I draw upon a diverse set of methods, blending interviews, social network analysis of employment data, participant analysis, and textual analysis of industry publications, professional awards, and conferences to make sense of how new skills and practices become entrenched throughout the profession of journalism. First, I created a data set of archival industry materials that includes trade publications, organizational documents, and job listings. I collected, reviewed, and analyzed the data set, which served as a starting point for tracking institutional change in journalist jobs, skills, roles, and expertise. Archival industry materials are ideal for uncovering processes of institutional change,[94] and trade publications and industry documents are specifically often used as a data source as they provide a window into the developments and dynamics necessary for conducting institutional analyses.[95] Analysis of over 320 industry documents and 8,000 listings of journalism job openings shows the destabilization and deinstitutionalization of established professional journalism practices (Chapter 2), experimentation and evaluation of news nerds (Chapter 3), legitimization of news nerds (Chapter 4), and diffusion of news nerds (Chapter 5) over the decade-long period (as mentioned, 2011 to 2020). An analysis of a corpus of programs from three annual professional journalism conferences (2011 to 2020) complements the findings in Chapter 3 on the evaluation of news nerds, and an analysis of prestigious journalism award winners over the last decade complements the findings in Chapter 4 on legitimatization of news nerds.

Second, I conducted interviews with 23 news nerds over the past four years. Initial interviewees were strategically identified based on a wide network of professional contacts; subsequent subjects were identified based on recommendations from the initial interviews. Interviewees were generally representative of a wide range of organizational sizes and functions. I conducted all interviews on the record, although interviewees were offered the option of anonymity. In addition, my participant observation at various news nerd conferences and industry meetings provided invaluable context and contacts from which to study this phenomenon.

Third, I created a unique data set of journalist employment histories to conduct a network histories analysis.[96] Network histories refer to a novel method that emphasizes the use of a social network perspective paired with digital trace data of employment histories to examine how hiring patterns, producers of communication, and organizations are evolving over time.[97] Based on a sample set of news organizations (for methodology behind the sample set and summary data of the news organizations, see the Data and Methods Appendix), employment histories (and other pertinent information) on professional journalists were created by aggregating public social-networking data. Position job titles, organizations, and dates of employment were collected for the employment histories of each employee at the sample news organizations. Educational information including undergraduate degree and graduate degree (when applicable) was also collected for each employee. Organizations and positions in the data set were categorically coded in order to summarize the data. Immediately following completion of collection and recording, data were de-identified and anonymized.

Employment data were collected to recreate the employment patterns of individuals working for those organizations, which allows for analysis of the organizational, educational, and skill-set trajectories of modern professional journalists. Employment data lend themselves to social network analysis (SNA),[98] which is widely used in studying the composition of a workforce over time. More specifically, SNA enables the examination of a connection between two entities based on a common relationship, which in this case, illustrates the movement of professionals between different positions, organizations, and industries and thus provides insight into the hiring and employment patterns of news nerds within the overall journalism network. In total, this unique data set includes 3,587 journalists[99] employed at 11,117 jobs, 3,303 different organizations, and 8,749 instances when an employee left one company and went to work for another company.

The visualization in Figure 1.1 illustrates an example of the data and analysis possible with network histories. Here, you can see the overall employment network in aggregate over time. The visualization provides a snapshot of the organizations that are most central in the network, as well as those that occupied a more peripheral role. Organizations such as ABC News, NBC News, and the Huffington Post occupy central positions as many employees pass through these organizations during their careers working in New York City news organizations. Organizations such as MTV, Vice, and Al Jazeera also occupy important

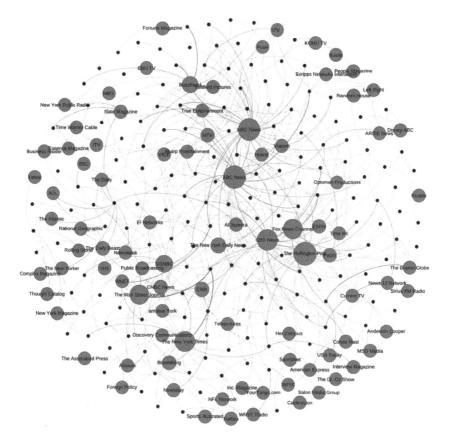

Figure 1.1 Visualization of job by news organization (2011–2015). Journalist jobs beginning each year (2011–2015) are represented by black nodes, and news organizations are represented by blue nodes. Journalist nodes are uniformly sized, and news organization nodes are sized according to degree. Traditional journalist jobs are represented by gray edges connecting journalists to organizations; news nerd journalist jobs are represented by pink edges forming the connection. If a journalist has multiple jobs within the same organization that are mixed (news nerd and traditional), the edge is colored green. Transitions to a new position within the same company are indicated with thicker edge connections. The diagram is filtered to show only those nodes with five or more connections (degree > 4) to aid in clarity of visualization. The Fruchterman Reingold algorithm was applied to create this layout.

positions at the center of this network, which indicates that they have a lot of employee crossover with the sample news organizations.[100]

This dataset serves as the primary case study for the entire book—a systematic analysis of modern journalism employment patterns. The case study is used to quantitatively highlight the role of news nerds within the overall journalism employment network, their career paths, and their corresponding educational background and skills.

2

Destabilization of Established Journalism Practices

There was a fundamental change to the information economy. It
was literally a tectonic plate of civilization moving . . . To me, it's like
there's a couple pieces to it: there's the one end of here is the rival to
the print distribution monopoly. So, you know, working in a newspaper this long and I've come to realize that so much of it was based
upon the ability to put this hunk of paper on people's doorstep—that
was the only way to get classified ads and the only way to get coupons
and the only way to get movie listings. And so, there was this regional
monopoly of advertising distribution. And now, there are new competitors to that, thanks to new technology. And those new competitors have won, which is, I guess, the short way to say it. And now we
have to have a different kind of business that is not based around
scarcity. Instead, it's based around, well, I don't know—we think
now, digital subscriptions. And then so, advertising has changed, the
distribution model has changed, and the competitive landscape has
changed, along with it.[1]

The above quote from news nerd Ben Welsh, editor of the Data and Graphics
Department at the *Los Angeles Times*, reveals the underlying dynamics of what
organizational scholars Royston Greenwood, Roy Suddaby, and C. R. Hinings
call *deinstitutionalization*.[2] Greenwood et al. use this term to describe the forces
in the external environment of an industry—be they social, technological, regulatory, or political in nature—that have the power to instigate profound change.
External events "jolt" and destabilize established practices of an industry creating an opportunity space that precipitates the entry of new players, who in effect
disturb the taken for granted by introducing new ideas and the possibility of
change.

In applying this line of reasoning to the case of news nerds, it is clear that we
need to think about how the overarching economic, technological, and social

News Nerds. Allie Kosterich, Oxford University Press. © Oxford University Press 2022.
DOI: 10.1093/oso/9780197500354.003.0003

changes influenced the news industry in general and more specifically, the profession of journalism. In particular, given that the focus is on a specific decade of development in the profession of journalism (2011–2020), we need to identify those general features of the U.S. economy that impacted the news industry. In addition, we need to understand how changing social conditions during this time could have opened an opportunity space for the entrance of new players into the industry. In other words, the question at hand is how did the wider environmental context change during this time period in ways that made possible the development of news nerds?

In this chapter, I focus on the interaction between the news industry and the wider environmental context, including broader economic and social trends, within which the profession of journalism operates. In doing so, this chapter takes an in-depth look at the economic, technological, social, and political changes that occurred external to the news industry that then destabilized the established practices of the profession. I identify several key technological developments such as the growing ubiquity of the internet, cloud computing, and mobile and social platforms that continue to influence the rise and spread of digitalization and connectivity, which coupled with associated economic realities and social changes such as those related to news consumption behaviors have jolted the established practices of the news industry and thus the status quo regarding what it means to be a professional journalist.

Through firsthand accounts provided by industry practitioners coupled with trade press coverage and industry documents, the chapter illustrates how these changes created an opportunity space for the entrance of new players outside the traditional boundaries of the news industry. New entrants in the form of, for example, tech-centered digitally native news organizations and software programmers offered an alternative approach to the established practices and processes of the profession of journalism. Through analysis of the employment histories of the case study of professional journalists, I further illustrate how these new entrants brought new skills and expertise to the profession. In sum, new entrants ignited the possibility of change and led to further deinstitutionalization of the profession of journalism.

Economic Realities

While the news industry has long dealt with changes in technology (e.g., the introduction of radio in the 1920s and television in the 1950s), newspaper readership and revenues tended to remain largely stable.[3] It wasn't until the late 1990s that core business models of newspapers began to change as news organizations started experimenting with content uniquely developed for online distribution.[4]

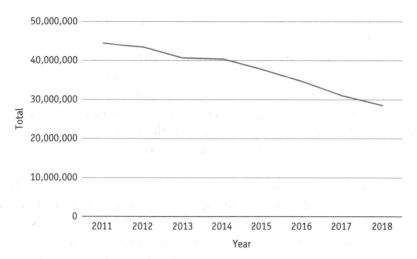

Figure 2.1 Total circulation of U.S. daily weekday newspapers, 2011–2018. Data in this figure are based on information from the Pew Research Center, which is available at https://www.jou rnalism.org/fact-sheet/newspapers/. Pew researchers used data from Editor & Publisher to determine the total circulation from 2011 through 2014. To determine the total circulation for 2015 onward, they analyzed the yearly change in total weekday circulation using Alliance for Audited Media data and applied percentage changes to the previous year's total. Alliance for Audited Media data includes only daily U.S. newspapers that report average Monday–Friday weekday circulation.

The reference to readership and revenue is crucial as the role of economics is central to understanding how the profession of journalism changed over time.

Figure 2.1 shows the total circulation of U.S. daily weekday newspapers, and Figure 2.2 shows the total combined advertising and audience revenue for U.S. newspapers. Both graphs, based on data from the Pew Research Center, show downward trends for the time period under study. In 1990, total daily newspaper circulation was 62.3 million; however, since 2011, total daily newspaper circulation has fallen by more than 39% from 44.4 million to an estimated 28.6 million in 2018.

Revenue, on the other hand, remained relatively steady through 2011— mostly due to a bubble in advertising revenue during the first decades of the internet and the rise of online news, despite a decrease in audience revenue.[5] Since 2011, however, total revenue (advertising and audience combined) for U.S. newspapers has decreased by about 32%. As shown in Figure 2.2, combined revenue from advertising and subscriptions decreased from $37.1 million to an estimated $25.3 million in 2018.

The numbers paint a similarly bleak picture for the profession of journalism when looking at the employment trends. Figure 2.3 shows three separate trend lines based on data from the Pew Research Center. First, the figure illustrates total newsroom employment in the United States from 2011 through 2019. In

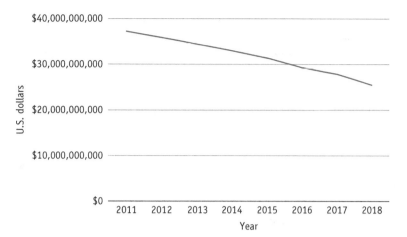

Figure 2.2 Combined advertising and circulation revenue of the U.S. newspaper industry. Data used in this figure are based on information from the Pew Research Center, which is available at https://www.journalism.org/fact-sheet/newspapers/. Data in 2011 and 2012 are from the News Media Alliance. Data from 2013 onward are based on Pew researchers' analysis of financial statements from publicly traded U.S. newspaper companies. Yearly percentage changes for these companies were calculated and then applied to the previous year's revenue totals.

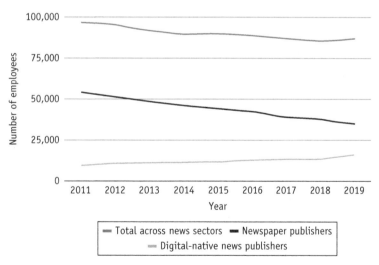

Figure 2.3 Newsroom employment at U.S. newsrooms, 2011–2019. Data used in this figure are based on information collected from the Bureau of Labor Statistics Occupational Employment Statistics and analyzed by the Pew Research Center. It is available at https://www.pewr esearch.org/fact-tank/2020/04/20/u-s-newsroom-employment-has-dropped-by-a-quarter-since-2008/.

addition, the figure takes a deeper dive into the data to highlight interesting disparities between the trend line for total newsroom employees in the newspaper publishing sector compared to that of total newsroom employees in the digital-native news sector.

As one can see, since 2011, employment in U.S. newsrooms has decreased by just over 9% from 97,000 employees in 2011 to 88,000 employees in 2019. Interestingly, when solely looking at newspaper newsroom employment, the loss is much more striking—an almost 30% decrease from 54,050 employees to 37,900 employees in 2018. During that same period, however, employees in digital-native newsrooms actually increased 69% from 9,520 employees in 2011 to 16,090 employees in 2019. In sum, total revenues for the news industry are down and the exclusivity of the profession of journalism is increasingly challenged.

Technological Developments

Economic trends are not the only external influence impacting the profession to journalism. It is important to note that professional journalists have been experimenting with technology to do their jobs for a long time. In 1952, CBS News used a Universal Automatic Computer (UNIVAC) to analyze election returns against past results and forecast Dwight D. Eisenhower as victor in the presidential election.[6] Computers were then used by newsrooms to aid in non-journalist work routines such as accounting, circulation, and production; later in the 1960s, computers began to pop up more frequently in newsrooms with the birth of computer-assisted reporting (CAR).[7]

Similarly, professional journalists have used data in their stories since the early days of reporting and have worked with databases and algorithms since the late 1960s, also in the realm of computer-assisted reporting.[8] Further advances in computing fostered journalists' adopting technology that created the opportunity for data integration into news production processes.[9] Shortly after that, journalist Philip Meyer published his landmark social scientific analysis of quantitative data to tell the story of the 1967 Detroit riots, pioneering a movement known as *precision journalism.*[10]

Since then, however, the growing ubiquity of digital technologies and data sources furthered the rise of "big data." Indeed, the "streaming, structuring, and storing of this information in reusable formats . . . is increasingly the raw material of journalism."[11] The coupling of this data with rapid computational advances facilitates and enables the analysis and visualization of public life in unforeseen quantities and detail. The impact of these technological jolts is increasingly evident throughout the news industry as professional journalists are required to develop new skills to tell stories and engage with readers in new ways.[12] Business models are changing to reflect the ways data can be utilized as a "raw material for profit, impact, and insight, co-created with an audience that was formerly reduced to passive consumption."[13]

The rapid proliferation of big data and advances in computing technologies represent only part of the technologically disruptive process affecting the news industry. Perhaps even more important is the growing influence of platform companies such as Facebook (Meta), Snapchat, Google, Apple News, and Twitter. The "platform era," as Emily Bell and her research team at Columbia University's Tow Center for Digital Journalism call it, represents these companies' rapid takeover of traditional news organization processes— processes that go beyond distribution to include control over what content audiences actually see and who gets paid for that attention.[14] The Tow Center research team issued several reports assessing the relationship between platforms and publishers, which began with the premise that the massive audiences offered by platform companies would lead to meaningful revenue for the news organizations. As time went on, news organizations continued to push their content to these platforms without any consistent financial returns. As platform companies became more explicitly editorial, Bell and her colleagues found a significant departure in the tone of news publishers' attitudes toward the technological development and the relationship with platform companies. According to their latest report, news publishers were more openly distrusting toward platforms than ever before and instead focused on regaining control of their revenue streams.[15]

It is, of course, worth noting that journalism grappled with online platforms (e.g., GeoCities) decades prior to the advent of Facebook and Twitter.[16] In contrast, however, today's platforms have evolved past their role as community forums and distributors to become gatekeepers and mediators of the content that audiences see. Third-party platforms often use algorithms, software, and other mechanisms to bring news content to consumers, acting neither as "neutral pipes, nor full media companies" but instead as "gatekeepers, controlling information flows, selecting, sorting, and then distributing information."[17] These organizations are commercial companies with values that don't necessarily align with the traditional foundations of the journalism profession and the Western notion of a free press.

The absence of public knowledge regarding what happens during the process between the creation of news and the consumption of news raises broader issues for democracy.[18] Indeed, how these platforms operate are economically sensitive, proprietary, and generally opaque. News organizations continue to cede control of publishing as a core activity and push content to these third-party platforms without guarantee of economic benefits.[19] These changes have a profound impact on the news industry and professional journalists as control of distribution, user access to news, and editorial judgment shifts to platforms that yield an increasing amount of power over the news ecosystem.

For instance, Facebook's average valuation (market capitalization) is approximately $332 billion since going public on May 18, 2012, compared to that of *The New York Times*, which averages $2.98 billion during the same time period.[20] These market capitalizations are, of course, simply one indicator of growth in social media platforms compared to the publishing companies of the news industry; however, they provide a hint at the economics of the relationship between news organizations and third-party platforms. According to Bell et al., the development of social media platforms has indeed had a greater effect on the U.S. news industry than the development of the internet, forcing news organizations to reevaluate traditional business models, production processes, and organizational structures.[21]

Social Changes

Along with technological developments related to mobile and social platforms come social developments regarding the ways audiences find and consume news. News consumption is increasingly mediated, delivered, and curated by third-party platform companies on mobile devices. According to a 2019 survey executed by the Pew Research Center, 57% of U.S. adults often get news on their mobile device—up from 21% in 2013.[22] Of course, coupled with this growth in mobile consumption is the growth in social media for accessing news. According to a 2020 *Reuters Institute Digital News Report*, almost half of those sampled in the U.S. (48%) get news via social media—almost double the amount in 2013 when only 27% of respondents consumed news this way.[23]

Audience fragmentation exists across a growing range of distribution and publishing platforms. While news consumers have increased access in terms of their choice of news outlets and the speed with which they access news, news organizations struggle with the fact that consumers access content not only through traditional distribution (e.g., organizational products such as print newspaper, online news website, television program, etc.) but also via third-party platforms and aggregators. Such circumstances led to efforts to evolve in order to meet the demands of a "digital-savvy consumer base who require information being presented in unique, digestible and sharable ways"[24] and as such, so too are efforts to evolve required of the professional journalists who produce that content.

Finally, an analysis of the recent jolts and disruption external to and within the news industry is insufficient without a discussion of trust. To be specific, journalistic authority, which Matt Carlson defines as "journalism's right to be listened to," is at an impasse.[25] While journalism has long struggled with public opinion, the crisis in authority specifically is arguably more prominent now than ever. This is due in part to ongoing change in the technological, economic, and political structures discussed, compounded by changes in the expected ways that the profession produces and audiences consume media. As new technologies are introduced into the media environment, new forms of media are produced, new norms regarding who can create media emerge, and understandings of news as a professionally produced product evolve.

The evolution of digital media, and the various platforms within, contribute to an overloaded environment of news stories claiming authority as explanations of the world. As such, audiences must confront—and often, question— the authority of this complex media environment each and every day. As the number of people who consume news on social media platforms increases, for example, so too does the number of people who distrust that news. According to the *Reuters Institute Digital News Report*, only 14% of survey respondents trust the news they read on social media.[26] Decline in trust of news goes further than those consuming news on social media platforms. In general, only 29% of U.S. adults surveyed trust the information they get from news overall, which is down from 32% in 2015.[27]

In sum, environmental jolts destabilized the established practices of the profession of journalism. Lack of trust in the institution of journalism, combined with economic realities, technological developments, and social changes in the ways people find and consume continue to substantially disrupt the established practices of the profession and the U.S. news industry at large. The changing realities of the news industry require organizations to reevaluate traditional news processes and practices, and in particular, those processes and practices related to the roles and responsibilities of professional journalists.[28]

Early efforts to adapt to digital disruption by the news industry were generally unable to keep pace with changes in technology and associated news consumption behaviors.[29] In fact, many of the changes that undermined traditional news processes and practices actually served as disruptive shocks creating an opportunity space for alternative approaches and the emergence of new players. Take, for example, the introduction of the iPhone (in 2007) and the increased availability of internet access, which facilitated an anytime, anywhere media environment. These developments indeed set the stage for a surge in the emergence of new players such as digital-native news organizations that catered specifically to the anytime, anywhere media conditions.[30]

Emergent Organizations

The circumstances laid out above interact to destabilize the taken-for-granted processes and practices of the profession of journalism and the news industry at large. Such destabilization helped create an opportunity space for the emergence of new players to enter the field. One emergent player, for example, came in the form of digital-native news organizations that emerged and developed entirely online. The reference to digital-native news organizations is important as the role of these new entrants in the news industry at large is central to understanding how the profession of journalism changed over time, especially with regards to the rise of news nerds.

Figure 2.4 shows the average number of business establishments each year for the newspaper publishing sector compared to the internet publishing sector according to data from the U.S. Bureau of Labor Statistics. As one might expect, there is indeed a slight downward trend in the number of newspaper publishing companies and a much more substantial upward trend in internet publishing companies. In fact, since 2011, the number of newspaper publishing companies in the U.S. fell by almost 16% from an annual average of 8,278 to 6,966 in 2019. Contrast that with the number of internet publishing companies in the U.S., which grew by more than 87% from an annual average of 9,088 in 2011 to 17,006 in 2019.

By definition, digital-native news organizations emerge and develop entirely online, differentiating themselves from traditional news organizations in a variety of ways. Built on and for the web, these organizations have technology at

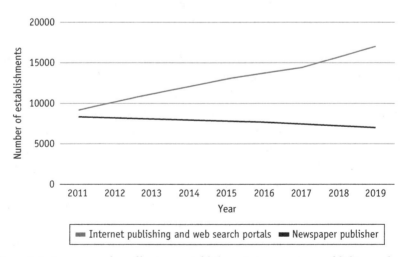

Figure 2.4 Average number of business establishments in newspaper publishing and internet publishing, 2011–2019.

their cores with systems and professionals dedicated to data, analytics, engineering, and content management.[31] Digital-native news organization Vox, for example, was designed with a custom-built content management system particularly well-suited for innovation in data and interactive news.[32]

As such, digital-native news organizations are typically agile and willing to experiment with new technologies that could potentially foster innovation. This innate flexibility is further facilitated by the difference in distribution of costs as compared to traditional news media organizations. As media and technology analyst Ben Thompson explains, the costs for a technology company, similarly to a digital-native news company, are mostly upfront: money is spent on salaries to develop the product, which can be used anywhere and for a long period of time, and it has minimal costs to produce copies, so the majority of revenue becomes profit.[33]

Furthermore, these digital-native news organizations are typically capable of quickly meeting the requirements of digital news audiences that increasingly demand easily accessible, unique, and engaging forms of news and information. Digital-native news organizations strive to innovate by creating new styles and forms of storytelling and hire journalists with new skills such as data visualization and audience analytics to do so.[34] As early as 2012, digital-native news organization the Huffington Post had an interactive news editor and a data scientist on staff.[35] NowThis, a digital-native news organization first launched in 2012, began with the mission and staff to produce video for mobile and social platforms.[36] In general, these new entrants are inherently capable of benefiting from social media as a contributor to content creation, distribution, and engagement.[37]

Lastly, it is also worth mentioning another organizational form as a new entrant to the news industry at large. Indeed, an additional consequence of the economic, technological, and social jolts outlined above is the rise of third-party web analytics companies. While news organizations have long collected data about their readers, the tracking, storage, and speed capabilities in the age of "big data" have made the process far more sophisticated. Third-party companies rooted in technology and analytics spaces entered the playing field of the news industry and began catering specifically to journalists with data used to measure performance and thus impact production.

The implications of these new entrants are profound and widely studied. Scholars have studied, for example, the ways in which web analytics have been adopted as metrics of success for content and audience engagement.[38] Web analytics companies have forced journalists to rethink their professional processes,[39] and, as such, journalists oftentimes find themselves in newsrooms that place more value on such data than on journalistic intuition.[40] In fact, journalism scholars Valerie Belair-Gagnon and Avery Holton found that to this day, web analytics companies deliberately position themselves as external disrupters to the news industry at large.[41] Indeed these new entrants are not fully on the inside bounds of the traditional profession of journalism.

Emergent Funding

Digital-native news organizations continue to gain traction in the wake of disruption that marked the news industry since 2011. Reinforcing the need for innovation and new business models, venture capital funding proved critical to the growth of these emerging players. While venture capital funding is essentially a provision of necessary external resources, it is discussed here as an example of another new entrant—an emerging and alternative method of funding within the news industry.

Take digital-news native BuzzFeed, for example, a company that received approximately $500 million in external funding.[42] Digital-native news organization Business Insider has raised over $50 million in external funding while TheSkimm has raised over $27 million in external funding. Globally, digital news companies raised a total of $781 million in funding in 2019, which was a 421% increase from $150 million in 2011. Figure 2.5 shows the amount of external funding each year raised by digital news organizations. As is evident, over the decade-long period of study, external funding in the digital news sector increased. External funding reached its peak in 2017 with a total of $1.67 billion raised by digital news organizations. This was followed by a general decline as venture capital funding began to trend away from the news industry at large.

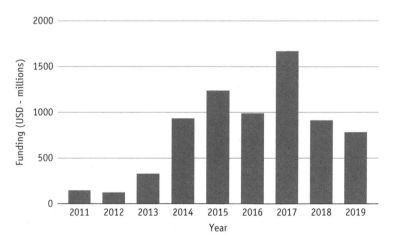

Figure 2.5 Total external funding in the digital news sector, 2011–2019.

It is worth noting that venture capital funding is not a cure-all for the challenges posed by digital disruptions to the news industry.[43] There are drawbacks and limitations to venture capital funding; yet, especially early on during the period of study, this new method of funding proved to be a significant resource for driving organizational innovation in the news media industry at large.[44] While venture capitalists will often drive a new organization in a particular direction or mold its growth in particular ways, it's possible that these directions may not be in line with the core vision of the organization. Nevertheless, venture-backed news media startup organizations were on the rise, and they continue to impact the dynamics of the news media ecosystem.[45]

Emergent Actors

In general, and since 2011 specifically, there has been a substantial increase in the number of new entrants in the news industry that have important ramifications for the profession of journalism. Digital-native news organizations emerged and introduced a number of innovations from outside the traditional boundaries of the news industry, while venture capital funding emerged as a new alternative to financing the profession. New entrants, however, also came in at the actor level—in the form of new professionals bringing new knowledge, experience, and expertise into the news industry.

In 2008, the Medill School of Journalism at Northwestern University partnered with the John S. and James L. Knight Foundation to create a scholarship program aimed at bringing web developers and programmers into news organizations to help solve problems and inspire innovation. The call for admissions to the program read:

> Are you a skilled programmer or Web developer? Are you interested in applying your talents to the challenge of creating a better-informed society? Do you want to learn how to find, analyze and present socially relevant information that engages media audiences? Do you see possibilities for applying technology as a way to connect people and information on the Web or new delivery platforms? If your answers are "yes," consider coming to Medill for a master's degree in journalism. You can earn your degree in just a year. You will learn new skills that will open doors to new opportunities that might help build a better democracy. And a new program at Medill offers you a chance to win a fully funded scholarship.[46]

Brian Boyer, who was the head of Product Operations at Spirited Media at the time of interviewing, and Ryan Mark, formerly a data editor and engineer at Vox, were awarded the first two scholarships. Neither of them had any journalism experience or even considered studying journalism. According to Boyer, he used to consider himself an outsider within the news industry as he began his career as a software developer with a degree in computer science and several years of professional experience building software for lawyers, banks, and finance companies:

> The work I was doing was work that left me unsatisfied. I liked the act of making, leading creative teams, but at the end of the day . . . I didn't feel like I was contributing to society. And so right around that time of being disillusioned, I happened upon an opportunity to study journalism—which I had never considered as a career—at Northwestern . . . and it kind took a very fast career turn, and I was like okay let's go to J-school.[47]

Upon completion of the one-year program at Northwestern, Boyer and Mark went on to the *Chicago Tribune* and created the first news applications team in 2009. Many of the founding members of this team came from similar backgrounds outside of news, joined by a common interest in open data. As Boyer went on to explain about the early team:

> What we had in common was an interest in open government and in open data . . . a lot of the people that we hired at the beginning were converts. And that was a matter of necessity. It wasn't me saying I don't want journalists, it's just there was a shortlist of people that we could have hired . . . it was *The New York Times* interactives team and then a handful of people around . . . some could code, but most were data nerds . . . We thought the Open Government was sort of the right, ya know, it was an easy conversion to say, hey data nerd, why don't you do this with a slightly different intent.[48]

But Boyer's story provides only a snapshot of the emerging alternatives to the profession of journalism given the broader scope of the industry. As Madi Alexander, data journalist at Bloomberg explains: "time outside the bubble is helpful." Job descriptions for journalist positions started to require the ability to code, and those with the ability to fulfill the position at the time were outsiders with fresh skillsets and new ideas.[49] "They were not the standard pick a lot of newsrooms choose," said Boyer.[50]

Jeremy Bowers, director of engineering at *The Washington Post*, echoes the applicability and regularity this pattern:

It wouldn't be that out of place for someone who was going to go work at Google to go work at the *LA Times*. It would be smaller and more mission driven, but the development environment wouldn't be that different. Your day-to-day work wouldn't be that different. And that's a far cry from where we were. Think about trying to say that with a straight face. And I know that's true of the *Times*, the *Post*, and the *Journal*, and I bet there are others that are similar.[51]

Since Boyer and Mark, about 15 scholarship winners have graduated from the program to go on and work in the news industry.[52] Further collaborations developed between computer scientists and journalists often in the form of meetups and hackathons.[53] However, the news industry continued to struggle to find journalists who had data and developer skills in combination with the journalistic judgment necessary to produce successful and innovative news products.[54]

News nerd Ben Welsh (as mentioned, editor of the Data and Graphics Department at the *Los Angeles Times*) describes a similar outside-in trajectory into news nerdery with his "accidental introduction" to journalism that began with an experience as an assistant to two investigative journalists while a college student—at which point in time he had no journalism experience nor any ambition to become one:

> I was there as like, a lackey, which meant booking interviews and cutting tape and one day, filing my first public records request. I got back from a corrupt suburb of Chicago with this lengthy pile of legal bills and this huge print out and thought, "Well, how are we going to do the story?" And it was just like, "Well, we're going to add it all up." And so, I made my first spreadsheet and just spent a couple days typing in these dozens of pages of printouts into a spreadsheet so that we could it add up . . . And that was my first spreadsheet. That was my first data analysis story, and I didn't really even set out to do. It just kind of happened.

As a college student with new real interest in pursuing journalism, Welsh realized that having these computer skills could truly make a difference and support the news production process:

> As someone who is like totally unqualified to be there, it was kind of like a way I had in. You know what I mean. For someone like me who didn't have the traditional experience or skills, learning the computer stuff was a little niche for me. I saw that and it was kind of a shortcut

to work on more ambitious journalism . . . So, it was like a kind of light bulb kind of went off in my head. . . So I tuned in and had time to learn. I thought here's how people do it and here is where it's going. And then I kind of decided that I was going to get on that train. I knew I needed to get even webbier—I needed to go more in that direction. And so, then, that's what I did. I got into that jet stream of people who were saying, well, we're going to be the next generation who are going to take this stuff online.[55]

Three years after the inaugural class of Medill-Knight Fellows, another new organization emerged bringing new players into the profession of journalism from outside areas of the news industry. In 2011, OpenNews launched to form a network of developers, designers, journalists, and editors that work in journalism The network also served as home to the Knight-Mozilla Fellowships, which took coders from outside of the news industry and placed them in newsrooms for 10 months.[56]

According to Dan Sinker, the director of OpenNews at the time, the goal was to "activate some hackers' civic orientation to bring them into newsrooms, where they can reach a broad audience and help, in some small way, pull journalistic institutions closer to a digital orientation."[57] While the Fellowship closed in 2017, over the years, hundreds of people have applied for it and a total of 33 individuals have received the award.[58] Indeed, the Knight-Mozilla Fellowship represents the entry of new professionals offering a fundamentally different approach to news production.

With the advent of the web and the shift from print news to online news (1990s to early 2000s), the profession of journalism failed to recognize the opportunities and obstacles of technological developments as well as the associated changes in consumption behaviors.[59] Indeed, the news industry at large is often slow to evolve and laden with legacy business models, processes, and practices. With this latest wave of transformation, however, there is an awareness that change must occur, even if it is destined to come from outside the field.[60] Take for example, Nate Silver, a statistician whose blog FiveThirtyEight was licensed by *The New York Times* in 2010 and is now owned by ABC News. Following the developments associated with deinstitutionalization and the publicity surrounding other actors who came into the profession of journalism from outside the traditional bounds of the news industry, it seemed as though new entrants would continue to emerge to address the problems associated with the increasingly digital and networked media environment.[61]

Within the context of the news industry specifically, technological disruption such as the developments of digital, social, and mobile media, compounded by economic turmoil, made for extremely uncertain times.[62] Tension and changing market conditions are often stimuli for the possibility of emergent forms. As such, there is no dearth of recent scholarship on emergent and evolving forms in digital journalism.

The development of digital technologies provided an opportunity space for new actors with different skill sets and experiences to enter the field of journalism such as occurs in the case of Alfred Hermida and Mary Lynn Young's examination of BBC News Online, a team comprised of both journalists and technologists that reconfigured traditional journalistic practices.[63] Wilson Lowrey similarly found that outsiders with non-journalistic backgrounds entered the fray of news with the rise of visual journalism.[64] One can look back even further in journalism's history to see changing patterns of influence on journalistic norms with the 1930s emergence of photojournalists[65] or, later, bloggers.[66] Journalism professor Scott Eldridge frames these emergent actors as "interlopers," defined as a "subset of digitally native media and journalistic actors who originate from outside the boundaries of the traditional journalistic field, but whose work nevertheless reflects the socio-informative functions, identities, and roles of journalism."[67] Belair-Gagnon and Holton call them "strangers" or those who "did not belong in journalism from the beginning and are importing qualities to it that do not originally stem from the journalistic profession."[68]

Across this research, no matter the terminology used to categorize these emergent actors, scholars have continued to explore how journalists perceive and interact with these emergent actors—or outsiders. The dominating theme across this literature is the tendency for new actors with new areas of expertise to be met with resistance and tension in several important ways. First, as journalism scholar Barbie Zelizer illustrates with the introduction of photojournalism in the early 20th century, resistance manifests in the form of questioning whether new actors can properly fulfill the role of journalist.[69] Second, as Lowrey found in the case of the introduction of visual journalists, tensions emerge concerning subgroup status and the right to make decisions in the news production process.[70] Third, resistance comes in the form of devaluing an emergent expertise as non-journalistic, as is evident in the case of the emergent actors who work in newsroom web analytics.[71] There is indeed an increasing influence of actors that do not fit into the traditional definition of journalist, and yet they are still involved in the production processes of journalism.[72]

Case Study: Industry Origins of Emergent Actors

In the form of organizations, funding, and professionals themselves, new players entered the news industry from outside the traditional boundaries. They offered an alternative approach to the established practices and processes of the profession of journalism. In doing so, new entrants ignited the possibility of change and represented deinstitutionalization in the profession of journalism and the news industry at large.

In an effort to better understand these dynamics of institutional change in action, specifically as they relate to the entrance of new players and the deinstitutionalization of the journalism profession, it is helpful to examine the players involved using the case study of journalist employment data. In returning to the case study, I am able to generate journalism employment networks to examine the industries that serve as career precursors to news nerd positions. Specifically, I generate one-mode networks that visualize the relationship between the current industry of each news nerd job (at the time of data collection) and the industry of the job prior in the career history of that employee. The visualization network in Figure 2.6 represents the relationship of industries from news nerd job to news nerd job aggregated over time (2011–2015).

The visualization in Figure 2.6 provides an overview of the industries and sectors involved in the development of news nerd jobs for the case study of professional journalists. In the aggregated industry network of news nerd jobs to news nerd jobs, one can see that marketing is the darkest blue and thus has the greatest number of outgoing connections to other industries. However, when one considers the weight of each edge (i.e., the number of connections to other industries multiplied by the weight of each one), print news, broadcast news, and digital-native news have the greatest out-degree scores (and thus the thickest edges in the visualization).

Out-degree centrality scores indicate the most central industries based on their feeding (outgoing) activity.[73] In other words, a higher out-degree centrality score indicates an industry from which more new news nerd jobs emanated. In aggregate, 34% of new news nerd jobs come from a different prior industry, and 51% of new news nerd jobs are journalists starting at a new organization. This indicates a small, but noteworthy, migration from other areas of expertise for new news nerd jobs.

Industry Origins of News Nerds Over Time

Examining the case study's journalist employment network on a year-by-year basis as opposed to in aggregate enables a deeper dive into the data in an effort to identify those industries that are most central for news nerd development over time. Table 2.1 provides a summary of the top three most central industries based on out-degree centrality within the network each year. Degree centrality

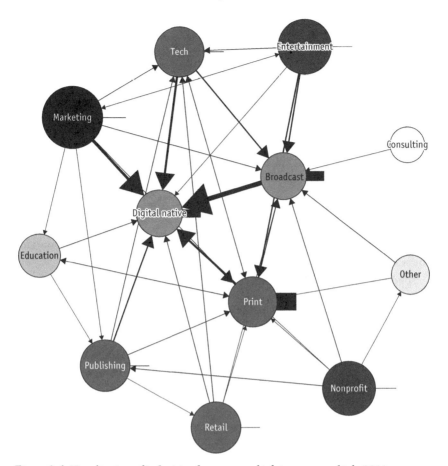

Figure 2.6 Visualization of industries for news nerd job to news nerd job, 2011–
2015. This visualization illustrates the movement of news nerd jobs to news nerd jobs among
industries in aggregate from 2011 through 2015. The current industry for each news nerd job is
included and a directed tie is present to connect from the industry of the prior news nerd job.
Industries nodes are sized and colored by out-degree (i.e., a bigger and darker blue node has more
outgoing connections when not accounting for edge weight). Connections are also sized according to
edge weight, and self-loops are included. The Fruchterman Reingold algorithm was applied to create
this layout.

scores were normalized, and edge weights were considered in all cases to control
for network size and to allow for comparison.

Within the industry network of news nerd job to news nerd job, print news
and broadcast news remain the most central and influential in terms of their outgoing activity. In other words, these news sectors are consistently the biggest
feeders of those employees moving from one news nerd job to another news
nerd job. Marketing, entertainment, and technology, to a lesser extent, each play
a central role as feeder industries between 2011 and 2014. By 2015, the news

Table 2.1 **Out-degree centrality for top industries (news nerd job to news nerd job).**

2011		2012		2013		2014		2015	
Print news	0.63	Print news	0.88	Broadcast news	0.80	Print news	1.75	Print news	1.82
Broadcast news	0.50	Broadcast news	0.38	Marketing	0.50	Broadcast news	1.38	Digital news	1.36
Entertainment	0.38	Marketing	0.25	Print news	0.50	Tech	0.75	Broadcast news	1.36

industry is responsible as the top three central feeders of employees moving from news nerd job to news nerd job.

Together these findings indicate that—over time—news nerd jobs are driven from within the news industry rather than drawing on expertise from outside the industry in other areas such as technology. On the one hand, this means that news nerds are being hired from within and are thus more likely familiar with existing tenets of the profession of journalism. On the other hand, this can also suggest that as the institutional change process progresses, news nerd hires are not necessarily bringing a fresh perspective to a given job. In other words, while early hires came from external industries, which may have accelerated the institutional change process, current news nerd hires reinforce the existing practices of journalism and the institutional influence of routines. This decrease in diversity of industry experience over time is indeed reflective of the rapid institutional change that has occurred and further supports the idea of institutional augmentation and the coexistence of both traditional journalists and news nerd without displacement or failure.

Summary

In this chapter, I analyzed deinstitutionalization in the profession of journalism in two phases. First, precipitating jolts in the external environment such as economic, technological, and social changes destabilized the established practices of the profession and the news industry at large. Second, such destabilization created an opportunity space for players outside the traditional boundaries of the news industry to enter the field. In the form of organizations, funding, and professionals themselves, new entrants offered an alternative approach to the established practices and processes of journalism and ignited the possibility of change within the profession. In analyzing industry origins of journalists in the case study, I show that indeed early news nerds were driven from industries external to news; however, as time went on, news nerds were coming from within the industry—a transition reflective of the institutional augmentation argument at large.

Although we are far from understanding why and how news nerds developed as an augmentation within the profession of journalism, we now have a good idea of how the broader environmental context matters for institutional change. The question of the next chapter is what happened within the news industry itself to enable the development and integration of news nerds within the profession of journalism? To answer this question, Chapter 3 will explore the initial experimentation and evaluation of extant news organizations as they respond to the challenges associated with meeting the needs of technological and social disruption and producing more innovative, accessible, and engaging content.

3

Experimentation and Evaluation
in the Profession of Journalism

An influx of outsiders is a common initial stage in institutional change and an apparent strategy throughout the news industry as the profession of journalism grappled with and responded to the digital turn. For news nerd Erin Medley, who was the director of editorial and audience development at New Jersey Advanced Media at the time of interviewing, however, it wasn't a strategy that proved successful. As Medley explains while recalling her experience hiring for her team in the newsroom:

> The person that we hired did not have a background in journalism . . . she didn't come to us from a journalism job . . . she had more of the social media background, but not necessarily for a news publisher. If it's a news organization, you need to have good news judgment, that's number one. Number two, you need to have excellent writing skills . . . it should be a seasoned journalist with a strong digital background.[1]

Echoing Medley's experience, an anonymous news nerd explains how "frustrating" it was early on when hiring news nerds who did not come out of a journalism program "because it was very hard to instill a kind of passion or curiosity for the news."[2]

Indeed, during the earlier years of the institutional change process (i.e., the early end of the 2010 decade), it was especially rare to find someone who had great journalistic skills and great news nerd skills. When people came in from outside the news industry to fill news nerd positions, they first came in from areas that valued analytics and coding skills. Such a scenario "created friction at the beginning of the evolution."[3]

As the institutional change process progressed, however, discussions started popping up throughout the news industry regarding data and apps, as well as

News Nerds. Allie Kosterich, Oxford University Press. © Oxford University Press 2022.
DOI: 10.1093/oso/9780197500354.003.0004

journalism as "more than just writers writing and editors editing."[4] And successful newsrooms started to find ways to combine these skills to produce this type of news in teams, explained news nerd Julia Wolfe, senior editor of data visualization at FiveThirtyEight.[5] Another anonymous news nerd managed an ad hoc team, for example, that consisted of both developers and traditional journalists. This enabled a combination of people with "strong journalistic sensibilities who understand ethics" and "good critics, as well as good sort of observers of the kinds of things that are being done today within the realm of journalism."[6]

So, what was happening at this point that prompted discussions throughout the news industry about what it means to be a professional journalist, what skill sets are necessary to make up effective newsroom teams, and what technological tools are used to do the job? As the previous chapter makes clear, timing and context matter. Economic, technological, and social changes in the external environment can influence what it means to be a professional journalist. The focus of this chapter, however, moves away from the broader external environment and looks inward to the news industry.

In order to understand how the profession of journalism undergoes institutional change, we, of course, also need to look at what is going on inside the news industry. This chapter thus examines two broad categories of development within the news industry: experimentation and evaluation. Organizational scholars Royston Greenwood, Roy Suddaby, and C. R. Hinings refer to this experimentation and evaluation stage as preinstitutionalization,[7] and they describe it akin to habitualization, which according to scholars Pamela S. Tolbert and Lynne G. Zucker "involves the generation of new structural arrangements in response to a specific organizational problem or set of problems, and the formalization of such arrangements in the policies and procedures of a given organization."[8]

Thus, in this chapter, I begin by providing an overview of news organizations' initial experimentation with news nerds as an alternative to what was considered to be within the traditional boundaries of the defined profession of journalism. Experimentation consists of those activities that can be identified as generating new structural arrangements by an organization in order to respond to a specific organizational problem or set of problems. This type of experimentation is a crucial component of institutional change and is evident in the way that news organizations temporarily test the boundaries of their departments and of their professionals. Within this category, for example, are (1) shifts made at the organizational level and (2) shifts made at the actor level. Here, we can once again turn to the data set from the case study of professional journalists to systematically investigate early experimentation in news nerds and those organizations that were leading the way in integrating news nerds into their newsrooms.

Next, I explain the consequential early evaluation of news nerds by extant news organizations as they respond to the challenges associated with meeting the needs of technological and social disruption and producing more innovative, accessible, and engaging content. This second category includes those activities taking place within the profession of journalism and the news industry at large that occur primarily to serve as evaluations of the utility of news nerds (and their output) and, nonetheless, facilitated growth in the development of news nerds themselves. Serving as examples of within the profession evaluation are three different industry conferences and symposia dedicated to various activities of consequence to news nerds. With a corpus of textual data from the programming of these conferences over the years of 2011 to 2020, we are able to see the changing prevalence of news nerd topics within the evaluation of the profession of journalism as a whole.

Taken together, these examples of experimentation and evaluation constitute the major developments from within the news industry and the traditional boundaries of the field of journalism that fostered institutional change in the profession and furthered the development and creation of a space for the eventual legitimatization of news nerds.

Experimentation

In the early 2010s, experimentation by extant news organizations with regard to news nerds and their output was evident in a variety of ways. At the organizational level, for example, there were shifts in the boundaries of departments that allowed for innovation labs or intrapreneurial efforts. Experimentation was also evident in the actual early hiring and integration of news nerds into the newsroom or assigning individual journalists to work on news nerd–related production. At the actor level, experimentation came in the form of individual journalist's exploring new skill sets and knowledge forms steeped in technology domains.

EXPERIMENTATION AT THE ORGANIZATIONAL LEVEL

Early experimentation began when a handful of news companies started shifting their organizational structures and departmental boundaries in an effort to foster internal innovation, diversify revenue, and, essentially, remain relevant. Structural shifts came in the form of new innovation labs or intrapreneurship efforts within news organization. Structural shifts were also evident as news organizations started to dip their toes into the hiring of news nerds and the production of news nerd work.

Intrapreneurship and innovation labs. In an effort to remain competitive and meet the changing economic, technological, and social demands outlined in the previous chapter, newsrooms began to experiment with new organizational structures. One of the ways news organizations attempted to accomplish this was through the process of intrapreneurship, which is the embedding of startups—and startup culture, typically reflective of being more adaptive to change—within the newsroom.[9] Take, for example, *The Seattle Times*, which in 2012 decided to experiment by launching a news apps team tasked with creating new newsgathering tools and storytelling platforms situated in the middle of its newsroom.[10]

That same year, Quartz launched as a digital-first startup and spinoff from Atlantic Media, which in and of itself afforded them the opportunities to begin with a culture of thinking outside of the box. Quartz is a successful example of early experimentation with news nerds and new organizational structures. According to former ProPublica and NPR news nerd Tyler Fisher, Quartz "really rethought the relationship between product and newsroom," and their organizational chart is organized completely differently from anywhere else. Fisher, currently the deputy director of technology at News Catalyst, which is a project based at Temple University that helps news organizations become sustainable in the digital media environment, goes on to explain that the company pivoted six or seven times in the past years that they have existed. "And I think that's what's kept them going. If they got locked into the first iteration of it, they would be gone by now," he said.[11]

As a response to challenges created by changes in the ways that audiences consume news—in this case specifically, daily traffic increasingly made up of mobile audiences—the Guardian US created a mobile innovation lab in 2015. The lab was explicitly purposed to "explore the challenges faced by journalists in the mobile age and experiment with new ways of bringing stories to life on smaller screens." Per the press release, the team consisted of editors, producers, designers, developers, and reporters and is embedded within the Guardian's news operations.[12]

A few years later, BuzzFeed News launched an initiative called The Tech + Working Group, which is a collaboration between reporters and BuzzFeed's technology department that includes roles such as data scientists, engineers, and product managers. The team is tasked with the mission of spending 7% of their time to experiment and learn new things. According to Logan McDonald, site reliability engineer at BuzzFeed, the initiative began when BuzzFeed management "realized that there is a place for the Tech team to help with reporting" and wanted to foster an "experimental and collaborative workplace."[13]

In the broadcast sector, one can look to the case of *Curious City*, which is a radio series at WBEZ Chicago focused on audience engagement that asks listeners to ask questions about its city, as another example of early organizational experimentation into the work of news nerds.[14] Since its launch in 2012 as an experiment in intrapreneurship, *Curious City* stories remain some of WBEZ's most successful content.[15] Other pioneering examples include incubators and innovation labs launched at *The New York Times*,[16] the Philadelphia News Network and Digital First Media,[17] and the *Boston Globe*.[18]

Although it was initially an experiment in new ways to engage with the audience, *Curious City* grew into a popular source of content and spun off into its own media startup; however, not all the other projects were quite as successful. In fact, many of these early examples of experimentation in news nerd work no longer exist today. Indeed, as is often the case with experimentation and the introduction of something new into an organization, tensions tended to build between those established processes and change. The relevant takeaway here, however, is the understanding that these experiments serve as prime examples of news organizations' structural shifts and their initial efforts toward incorporating data, visualization, and interactive content— as well as the professionals who produce it—in an effort to better meet the changing economic, social, and technological demands of the broader media environment.

Early integration of news nerds. During the earlier part of the 2010 decade, in an effort to gain a better sense of the state of news nerds during this time of experimentation and early institutional change, Steve Myers, who was then the managing editor of Poynter, conducted interviews with 20 professional news nerds at organizations ranging from the *Chicago Tribune, Los Angeles Times, Providence Journal, Des Moines Register,* and *Dallas Morning News*, to the *Texas Tribune*, Talking Points Memo, and ProPublica. Some of these news nerds were one on a team of several, but many were the singular journalist of their kind in their respective newsrooms. At digital-native Talking Points Memo, for example, two newsroom developers created the innovative Election Night app in 2012. It was a stand-alone app built specifically for election coverage that used data from the Associated Press to provide results to users.[19]

In the broadcast news sector, early organizational experimentation with the integration of news nerds occurred at National Public Radio (NPR), for example, when the company decided to hire a developer-journalist in 2011 charged with bringing algorithms and data into news work and merging the fields of computer science and news.[20] At WNYC, news director John Keefe began experimenting with data and code in 2009. His efforts eventually led to WNYC's infamous 2012 NYPD stop-and-frisk investigation, which encouraged and led the newsroom to pursue further news nerd work.[21]

On the traditional print end of the media sector spectrum, news nerd Jeremy Bowers, director of engineering at *The Washington Post*, describes his early forays into news nerd experimentation at the *St. Petersburg Times*:

> I was a blog administrator, basically, but they gave me the title, "News Technologist" which sounded really great, and my job was to write templates for our movable type blog and to work with people to make their blogs better. Everything was blogs—blogs were very exciting back then. There were no engineering teams. They didn't have any power at that time. I believe at the *St. Petersburg Times*, there were maybe four to five developers working on the whole website. The web CMS was a tiny little appendage to the newsroom that took an occasional story from print and pushed it out to an HTML template in a flat file, and if you wanted to edit it, you just literally go to that folder where the file was, open it up in a text editor, save it, and it would work on the internet.[22]

At another print organization, news nerd Wilson Andrews, information designer at *The Washington Post*, used data visualization techniques to meet the evolving demands of news consumers; in 2011, he won two awards for his Investigative Guns project and stated that it was only the beginning for more creative possibilities in news.[23] And of course, no discussion of early organizational experimentation in news nerds is complete without mention of *The New York Times* and *Snow Fall*, which is perhaps the most famous example of early integration of news nerds and their work.

Snow Fall tells the story of an avalanche in Tunnel Creek, Washington, by integrating text with video, photos, and graphics. The storytelling package was deemed an "evolution in online storytelling," and it received almost 3 million visits and 3.5 million page views with as many as 22,000 users at any given time.[24] In forming a journalism team made up of professionals that included both traditional journalists and data scientists, *The New York Times* was able to produce an innovative story integrating motion, graphics, data, video, and text in a way that felt seamless to the user. According to one anonymous news nerd, *Snow Fall* represented a shift from newsrooms creating digital content in which the reader "just clicks around" to much more than that—to creating content that can change in its presentation and thus the reader's experience of the story.[25]

Snow Fall won a Pulitzer Prize and was lauded as it was "enhanced by its deft integration of multimedia elements" including extensive video, animation, and graphics.[26] According to journalism scholar Nikki Usher who wrote the seminal book on interactive journalism, *Snow Fall* was indicative of the rise of this new form of news and the integration of traditional, narrative journalist skills with new storytelling steeped in code and platform expertise.[27] "What made people so crazy about *Snow Fall*," explained an anonymous news nerd, "was that this giant scrolling story integrated motion graphics, graphs, video, and text in a way that was seamless to the reader, and, at the same time, it was epic enterprise journalism, and then it was the world's biggest stand-alone news brand that did it."[28]

A case study of organizational leaders. Indeed, *The New York Times* is often acknowledged as a leader in the world of news nerds and news nerd work. As Tyler Fisher explains:

> I hate to be the person who points to *The New York Times* like everybody, but if you look at how they are set up, they employ probably 100 [news nerds] across their graphics team, interactives team, and the product team itself. They have an outsized team even for the size of the organization in terms of the percentage of people who understand digital technology. Not just programmers, but designers, product managers, you name it. They have the lion's share of that group. And I think it shows in their product.[29]

Fisher goes on to clarify that in fact it's more common that legacy print organizations don't know what to do with news nerds. "You also look at Gannett and Gatehouse and it's hard to see how they even conceive of newsroom technology and whether they see it as valuable at all," he added.

In an effort to shed light on organizational leaders in action and to better understand which news organizations are leading the way in early experimentation with regards to integration of news nerds, it is helpful to return to the case study of journalist employment data. Once again, we can generate journalist employment networks from the employment data set that help visualize the relationship between news organizations and news nerd jobs. These networks allow for comparisons between legacy news organizations and new entrant organizations (i.e., at the time, digital-native news organizations) and capitalize on the differences between their hiring practices of news nerds to better understand the role of factors such as extant organizational experimentation in the overall institutional change process over time.

The employment network of professional journalists was thus analyzed in an effort to better understand which organizations are actually leading in the hiring of news nerd jobs over time. Figure 3.1 provides an overview of the employment network based on all news nerd jobs and corresponding organizations (2011–2015). All jobs that were coded as news nerd were collected and ties were

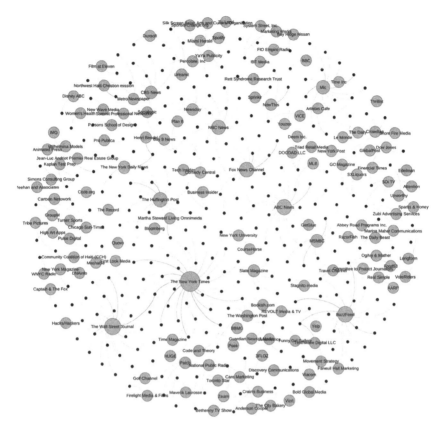

Figure 3.1 Visualization of news nerd job by news organization, 2011–2015. News nerd jobs beginning each year (2011–2015) are represented by black nodes, and news organizations are represented by blue nodes. Journalist nodes are uniformly sized, and news organization nodes are sized according to degree. All edge connections are colored in gray, and thickness corresponds with weight. The Fruchterman Reingold algorithm was applied to create this layout.

connected between journalists and organizations. In total, this network includes 373 jobs consisting of 153 journalists and 147 organizations.

As expected, the sample news organizations such as *The New York Times*, ABC News, and NBC News are most central within this aggregated network of news nerd jobs. Recall that centrality is the number of connections that a node has with other nodes within the network and can be used to indicate an organization's popularity, activity, or importance within a network. Aside from these central sample organizations, however, the visualization shows that Bloomberg, *Newsday*, and *The Washington Post* also occupy an important role within the news nerd network. This indicates that while these organizations are not at the center of the network, they do exert influence because of the flow of news nerd employees through these organizations.

Next, the networks for news nerd jobs were also analyzed on a yearly basis for a more nuanced comparison. Table 3.1 provides a summary of the top five most central organizations based on degree centrality within the network of news nerds each year from 2011 through 2015. Degree centrality scores were normalized, and edge weights were accounted for in all cases to control for network size and to allow for comparison.

Within the network of news nerd jobs, the most central organizations include an interesting mix over time. *The New York Times*, and to a lesser extent *The Wall Street Journal*, are consistently most central. Over time these organizations consistently hire the greatest number of new news nerds and implicitly may be viewed as industry leaders. In this case, centrality measures were based on degree centrality, which implies that these organizations are responsible for the most hiring and/or turnover of news nerds. The increasing presence of news nerd jobs at these organizations further indicates that this is the case—*The New York Times* alone was responsible for, on average, 14% of new news nerd jobs each year. This finding points to the importance of *The New York Times*, for example, as a training ground or hub for news nerds.

In 2011 and 2012, the most central organizations are a mix of print and broadcast news. Notably, two out of five of the organizations (*Newsday* and *Time*) are not part of the sample news organizations. This indicates that early institutional change in the profession of journalism, specifically regarding the hiring of news nerds, came from the periphery of the journalist employment network.

By 2013, digital-native news organizations began to play a more central role in the news nerd news network with the inclusion of BuzzFeed and Mic. In 2014 and 2015, two out of five of the most central news nerd organizations are digital-native news. Overall, as the institutional change process progressed, digital-native news organizations played more of a central role, reinforcing the

Table 3.1 **Top five organizations by degree centrality.**

2011		2012		2013		2014		2015	
New York Times	0.07	New York Times	0.08	New York Times	0.08	New York Times	0.11	BuzzFeed	0.16
Newsday	0.04	Wall Street Journal	0.05	Wall Street Journal	0.05	Huffington Post	0.06	New York Times	0.14
Time	0.04	ABC News	0.04	Fox News	0.05	Wall Street Journal	0.06	Wall Street Journal	0.11
Fox News	0.02	NBC News	0.03	BuzzFeed	0.02	BuzzFeed	0.05	ABC News	0.07
ABC News	0.02	MSNBC	0.03	Mic	0.02	NBC News	0.04	Mic	0.06

growing importance of digital-native news organizations in the New York City news nerd employment network as a greater number of news nerds moved through these organizations. In a practical sense, these findings further reinforce the importance of digital-native news organizations as leaders with regards to early experimentation and integration of news nerds themselves. This reflects their flexibility, adaptability, and overall ability to experiment and integrate new forms in the profession of journalism.

It's the news organizations that have experimented with news nerds and that have adapted to the digital world by adjusting and integrating news nerds into their newsrooms and everyday news production processes that continue to succeed. As news nerd Ben Welsh, editor of the Data and Graphics Department at *The Los Angeles Times*, explains:

> To me, the graphics profession has fundamentally changed in 20 years. It's just flipped on its head. You know, it was sort of a medium skill, specialized job in a sort of information factory. You know what I mean, it was like a little department in the information factory that could make four or five different types of charts, and it had its own assembly line and you needed specialized skills about how to make charts technically and a certain literacy . . . but, the graphics departments that haven't adapted from that are just gone. I think you could do a survey of graphics departments and you would find that almost every newsroom that is on that traditional model or that late 19th, 20th century model or whatever . . . I would say almost every one of them still on that model is gone. Like, it just doesn't exist. Like McClatchy just doesn't make graphics. And what's happened is the ones that have survived have fundamentally transformed these journalists—perhaps more than any other department in traditional newspapers—to be an independent news reporting department that reports and writes and designs and codes and publishes its own independent stand-alone pieces. There are now stand-alone, visual, substantial pieces that cover the major storylines that readers are jacked up to click on and read.[30]

Echoing Fisher's earlier assessment of *The New York Times*, Welsh continues by highlighting the *Times* newsroom and their leadership in news nerdery:

> *The New York Times* would probably be the prime premier example of this where you see these pieces with four or five charts together, and they tell the story of what happened at the debate tonight or what's going on with public opinion polls or who is Alexander Vindman and where does he fit in this like flowchart of the impeachment. And that

machine that makes those stories is a totally reformed, brand new assembly line that didn't exist at *The New York Times* 20 years ago . . And that requires the people in those departments to be independent and not to like be waiting to make things that stand-alone, that aren't accessories to go on someone's traditional print story. They use visual storytelling techniques, and then when they're most successful is when they really address the hot storylines and their strategic about the application of it, right, which *The New York Times*, I think is quite excellent at.[31]

As such, leading experimentation in news nerds evolved into true transformation of the core organizational processes—but, not only at the department level or the actor level itself—transformation must take place also at the management level as well. Successful experimentation and integration of news nerds requires a different type of editor. As Welsh explains:

It requires people to be show more initiative, to be better reporters, to be more aggressive, to be able to find and pin down their own stories that require them to have all of the technical skills. But it also requires a whole different type of editor who is able to assign and condition those things. It's like a big part of changing our graphics department has just been to say, "hey, we need editors." Because traditionally the attitude was "well the editor runs the metro department and you're going to make a chart for them, and the metro department is going to edit it. And you'll show the chart to the metro editor." But to do this independent news department thing, you have to be free of all those requests that come from the outside, and you have to have your own editing capacity to push things through.[32]

EXPERIMENTATION AT THE ACTOR LEVEL

As illustrated in Chapter 2, the early 2010s were an evolutionary moment for the profession of journalism and the news industry at large. Most of those working in early news nerd positions with roles steeped in data, analytics, and code came into the profession from the outside with a tech first (and journalism less so) ethos. According to an anonymous news nerd, while this created some friction between news nerds and more traditional journalists during the beginning of the evolution, that moment passed as news nerd roles became more integral to the business and news organizations increasingly integrated news nerd positions into their newsrooms. The fact is that "everybody obviously wants stories to be read as widely as possible and managers started to see that people with these [news nerd] skills are useful."[33]

At the individual level, the growth in social and digital technology spurred exploration and experimentation in journalism careers, especially for "tech-savvy young journalists."[34] For news nerd Rachel Schallom, who is the deputy editor of digital at Fortune Media but was a project manager at *The Wall Street Journal* at the time of interviewing, "journalism has always been the most important part." She goes on to explain that early in her career, she "worked with people who didn't care about the journalism," and when it came time to hire for her own team, a lack of journalism experience was a nonstarter.[35]

As another news nerd interviewee emphasized, "[journalism] experience is optimal . . . it's easier to teach tech skills than to actually teach journalistic sensibility." This news nerd goes on to explain:

> I also think it probably takes a commitment to teaching and reinforcing certain kinds of journalistic values, which are sort of—they're not in flux—but they are being challenged day to day. So, you know, would you put an emoji in a breaking-news alert? There are all kinds of questions where the need to speak to an audience, but an increasingly mobile and an increasingly younger audience sort of challenges the notions of what is acceptable and what isn't. And so, you need smart people who can actually represent some of the audience, but also understand how the new tools can be used in an effective way that isn't too over the top. So, you need someone who's going to understand when, yes, it is fine to put an emoji in a breaking news story.[36]

In fact, several news nerd interviewees emphasized the ability to experiment individually and learn news nerd-related skills on the job. According to Adam Playford, deputy editor of investigations at the *Tampa Bay Times*, he always felt he would have "a better shot at being able to program as a reporter than the other way around."[37] Indeed, news nerd skills like coding are "skill-based learning mechanism[s] and you can teach yourself how to do that" emphasized Sisi Wei, who at the time of interviewing was the deputy editor of news applications at ProPublica and is now the director of programs at OpenNews.[38]

Of course, individual experimentation with regards to news nerds goes hand in hand with the notion that for those journalists who entered the profession before or during any early institutional change, there was little to no guidance toward news nerdery within the training grounds of journalism schools. CJ Sinner, formerly a data graphics producer and now the data visuals editor at the Minneapolis *Star Tribune*, graduated from a journalism program that had yet to adapt to the emergence of the news nerd. Once out in the news industry, it quickly became clear to her "how much more potential there was that was not being tapped." She continued to explain that she "didn't even have the skills to understand how to start," and even after some time working as a professional journalist, "it's not always clear what skills are needed and what is the best use of time." According to Sinner, it was rare that management had answers to those questions either, and a lot of time during the early days of institutional change was spent figuring out "who we [news nerds] are and what we're doing."[39]

At the *Tampa Bay Times*, Playford is working to fix some of those challenges. He explains, "The path that I took to learn both programming and reporting didn't exist . . . Now, I'm trying to find ways to make those paths exist here."[40] In fact, there is a way to see news nerd skills as compatible with traditional journalist jobs. As Wei explains from her experience at ProPublica, journalists with certain backgrounds and positions can actually learn news nerd skills like coding easily because of aspects of their jobs that might not immediately seem related:

> We found that anyone who has a copyediting background does really well programming because they're already fine-tuned to paying attention to details in the actual letters and punctuation of words. And a lot of programming is getting those fine details of literally what you type and the punctuation that goes around it correct so the computer can actually understand the commands you're issuing. We also found that people who already do data journalism, people who are in the NICAR [National Institute for Computer-Assisted Reporting] community, they're already really interested in data analysis, and so for them, learning how to code either helps them accomplish their data analysis more quickly, or it allows them to do an interactive presentation of the analysis that they do.[41]

Shedding light on these connections highlights the utility of news nerd skills for traditional journalists, which contributes to the current drive of change from within the profession. Indeed, the position of a modern journalist is more than what was once considered as that of a traditional journalist and requires a broader skill set than your traditional "*His Girl Friday* reporter."[42] As Wei goes on to explain:

> Writing code and being able to understand data is integral to journalism as a whole. [Journalists] need to move in the same way that the world moves. Every industry is affected by big data right now, and if we can't understand it ourselves, we can't check what people are saying. These skills are accessible, which is so incredibly helpful, especially for an industry in which the main goal is to tell the truth. We need a lot of tools to do that.[43]

Numerous interview participants echoed the above sentiment and considered themselves journalists first. According to one news nerd, "A significant percentage of us went through some kind of journalism training or came up through some kind of newsroom. Most of our [news nerd] team comes from a print background."[44] Indeed, the general consensus of interview participants holds that as institutional change related to news nerds continued to progress, experimentation at the individual level was increasingly common and thus, strategy regarding change in the profession would be driven from within the industry.

Evaluation

Change from within the profession of journalism is also represented in how organizations began to evaluate the utility of this new form of professional journalist. During this early stage of institutional change (approximately 2011–2012), there were a number of different conferences and symposia devoted to various aspects related to the evaluation of news nerds. Industry associations such as the National Institute for Computer-Assisted Reporting (NICAR), the Online News Association (ONA), and the Society for Professional Journalists (SPJ) all held sessions at their annual conferences dedicated to discussion of topics related to news nerds.

NICAR, which is a subprogram of Investigative Reporters & Editors (IRE) that has been in existence since 1989, has a long history in the profession that moved increasingly toward a mission of understanding how to use data and computing technology in producing news. The 2011 annual conference was described as "a creative collision of words and nerds."[45] SPJ, which partners with the Radio Television Digital News Association (RTDNA), hosts an annual conference named Excellence in Journalism (EIJ) to provide journalists with training and networking opportunities. In 2011, the year of its inception, there were training sessions on "visual storytelling," "digital tools," and "integrating Web and newsroom teams into one operation." Furthermore, in 2011, the annual ONA conference had five general sessions dedicated to news nerds including "Cooking Up Tasty Apps" and "Once Upon a Datum: Telling Visual Stories." At the 2012 conference, data journalism was singled out as a key skill for professional journalists.[46]

In 2011, leaders in journalism, technology, and computation also came together at the Symposium on Computation and Journalism to discuss the role of computing technologies in the practice of journalism and the opportunities and challenges for professionals involved.[47] That same year, OpenNews launched its conference—SRCCON (pronounced source-con), which was the first event primarily dedicated to journalists who code. Together, these professional conferences served to evaluate the utility of news nerds, further helping create a community and validate the work of news nerds throughout the profession of journalism.[48]

Tracking Evaluation of News Nerds Over Time

One difficult challenge in understanding institutional change and specifically in this preinstitutionalization stage is how to depict and understand change in evaluation over time. Here, we can turn to the corpus of professional journalism conference programs to understand evolving depictions and evaluations of news nerds over the last decade (from 2011 to 2020). This corpus includes every conference program for the three major annual professional journalism conferences in the U.S. (ONA, NICAR, and EIJ). Using this corpus, we can identify key topics related to new nerds and plot their emergence and differentiation from one another. This enables the description of their changing prevalence and the tracking of their valuation over time. In doing so, we gain new insight into the ways the evaluation of news nerds has changed within the profession of journalism itself.

Indeed, an integrative aspect of institutional change is the extent to which people are exposed to new images, representations, and structures of meaning. In the case of the profession of journalism, one way news nerds are evaluated is through discussions at sessions at professional conferences. These within-profession events significantly contribute to the representation and understanding of the journalism profession, and they reflect the representations of the profession itself. Figure 3.2 plots the change in prevalence of the focal key topics related to news nerds. The y-axis, in other words, indicates share of all words in the corpus in each year allocated to each topic. The key topics of "data," "analytics," and "product" are accompanied by "journalist" to provide a comparison to a topic that is objectively common and established before the rise of news nerds.

Notably, very few words were devoted to any of the three focal new nerd topics (i.e., data, analytics, and product) before 2012. In 2011, the news nerd topics accounted for just about 0.61% of all words in the corpus. This changed substantially in 2012 when 3.46% of all words in the corpus were dedicated to news nerd topics with the largest share (3.13%) assigned to "data." By 2014, the news nerd topics reached their first peak comprising just about 3.81% of all of the words in the corpus. This marks a relatively sharp and rapid increase in the discursive attention paid to new nerds during the evaluation happenings of professional conferences. Although the balance among the new nerd topics changes, the

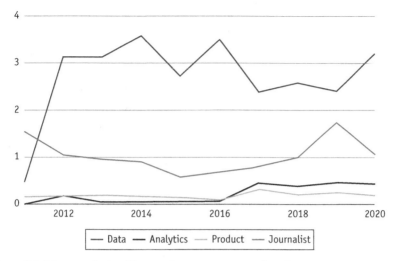

Figure 3.2 News nerd related keywords as a percentage of conference program corpus

share never falls below 2.92% (2015) and, in all other years, it hovers above that level and hits a second peak in 2020 when the total reaches 3.81%.

Another interesting observation from Figure 3.2 is that share of each news nerd topic remains relatively stable across the years. Most strikingly is that "data" is significantly more prominent a topic than the others across the decade. This is telling as the topic of data is such an integral part of the NICAR ethos to begin with—it makes sense that such a share would be allocated to evaluating its utility in the setting of the professional conference.

Summary

Together, the developments outlined in this chapter chart the beginning of extant news organizations' experimentation with and evaluation of news nerds and presents evidence for the relationship between the development of news nerds and change from within the news industry itself. In response to the challenges associated with meeting the needs of technological and social disruption, a number of extant news organizations began to experiment with and evaluate the potential of news nerds. Shifts in organizational structures, experimentation, and conference events are concrete reactions to the destabilization of established professional journalists and the news industry in general.

The case study of journalist employment networks provides further quantitative, statistical leverage to explain how news organizations experimented with news nerds by hiring and integrating these professionals throughout the process of institutional change. During the early stages of institutional change, traditional news organizations such as print and broadcast media hired a greater number of news nerds compared to digital-native news organizations. This pattern quickly reversed itself, shedding light on role of digital-native news organizations as leaders with regards to the hiring of news nerds, which further reflects the flexibility and adaptability to change of these newer entrants.

In studying the corpus of professional journalism conference programs, we are able to get a glimpse into the evolving prevalence of the evaluation of news nerds from within the profession over the last decade. Indeed, characterizing institutional change—specifically preinstitutionalization and change from within—can oftentimes be quite challenging. In focusing on topics relevant to the interest of news nerds, this analysis of a large corpora of textual data is a worthy complementary study of change in evaluation of news nerds over time.

It's important to note, however, that experimentation and evaluation of news nerds at this point were conducted on an ad hoc basis and not fully integrated into newsroom routines or business models. For instance, the use of data and analytics in editorial work to understand who is interacting with a story and to inform future coverage was still in its infancy.[49] There certainty wasn't any sense of legitimization or diffusion with regards to news nerds and the profession of journalism. For example, according to Matt Waite in 2011, a former news nerd at the *St. Petersburg Times* and current professor of journalism at the University of Nebraska:

> It's tempting to say that a real critical mass is afoot, marrying journalists and technologists and finally getting us to this "Future of Journalism" thing we keep hearing about. I've recently had a job change that's given me some time to reflect on this movement of journalism + programming. In a word, I'm disappointed.[50]

Indeed, experimentation and evaluation activities remained external and not central to business models, planning, and development. According to Gabriel Dance, interactive editor at The Guardian US:

> There's not any sort of editorial or reporting divide between my team and the rest of the newsroom . . . the people on my team, I call them "interactive journalists." But I'm looking forward to the day we can drop some of the prefixes and leave it as "reporter" or "journalist" . . . The way I see it, the web has evolved and changed the way we have the ability to tell stories. What we're doing is simply adapting to all these new ways we have to tell stories.[51]

And so, while Chapter 2 explores the impact of developments external to the profession of journalism and the news industry at large, this chapter presents evidence of developments occurring internally. At this point in the timeline of early institutional change (i.e., early 2010s), internal and external conditions clearly facilitated the development of news nerds throughout the profession of journalism. However, the full story of news nerds and institutional change requires reference to yet another factor. The legitimization of news nerds is thus the subject of Chapter 4.

4

Legitimization of News Nerds

I think just even a few years ago some of the tone of some of the discussions at conferences like the NICAR conference was like, "Oh I'm this one person working in the newsroom, and no one really knows what I do. How do I get them to support my interactive work or whatever." And that's becoming less and less of a thing now that people are getting the message that this is important. It's important to have somebody with data chops who will be a huge contributor to your newsroom, and especially when they can sit down elbow to elbow with a traditional reporter who is covering a beat and then enhance the work that they are doing.[1]

The above quote from an anonymous news nerd describes the beginning of the recognition of the importance and value of news nerds within the profession of journalism. As this news nerd goes on to explain:

> Oftentimes, people working with the data are the ones who are pitching and coming up with new stories. At my previous news organization, some of the biggest projects that were published over the last few years were ones that originated from the Visuals team [a news nerd team]. They weren't handed down to us, and that was a big dynamic that I saw change. For a long time, [news nerd teams] were kind of like Kinko's. Journalists in the newsroom would go, "hey can we get . . ." You know literally people would come over and be like, "can I get a color print out of this" or like "can you guys get some screen shots of this product from here?" And it changed to one where they saw what we were able to do.[2]

This news nerd describes a fundamental transformation in the recognition of news nerds from within the news nerds—a shift from a view of news nerds as a service desk to news nerds as legitimate, integrated journalists who were grounded in the work they did:

At my prior news organization, our team was working with the investigative reporters on the Medicare story, which won the Pulitzer Prize. And you know the reporters were on this, it was a 10-year effort with *The Wall Street Journal* to get this data released on Medicare Part B, but we sat down with the investigative team—who we had a great relationship with—and we were able to make this great, searchable interactive database that put a beautiful face on the whole thing. It let people and the reporters use the tool to find stories that they could get a report out as part of a larger series. So, we kind of earned a lot of respect by doing good work.[3]

Thus, while in the previous chapter, we saw how experimentation in news organization structures and journalism events helped spur the development of news nerds within the profession, this chapter is a continuation of that analysis that focuses on an examination of another crucial aspect of institutional change—legitimacy. Sociologist Mark C. Suchman defines "legitimacy" as the socially constructed general perception of appropriateness and taken-for-granted understanding of reality.[4] This definition makes it clear that central to the notion of legitimacy is a *socially constructed* perception or judgment, one manifested via actions such as acceptance or endorsement. The legitimacy of news nerds, therefore, is manifested as specific actions of alignment, approval, or endorsement. Suchman provides a breakdown of various manifestations of such alignment that we can examine to better understand the legitimization of news nerds such as moral legitimacy (i.e., normative approval), pragmatic legitimacy (i.e., self-interest), and cognitive legitimacy (i.e., comprehensibility and taken-for-grantedness).

In this chapter, I therefore set out to provide empirical evidence concerning the role of legitimacy of news nerds in the institutional augmentation of the journalist profession. This is accomplished through an analysis of industry documents, journalism award winners, and interviews with professional journalists, which show that news nerd legitimacy manifests morally, pragmatically, and cognitively.

The first task is to illustrate examples of the moral legitimacy of news nerds, such as the integration of news nerd–related journalism education programs into the norms of higher education journalism training and the integration of news nerds in news organization standards and culture. Next, I turn to the pragmatic legitimacy of news nerds, which is evident through the acknowledgment of the relationship between news nerd production output and financial benefits to news organizations. Finally, I discuss the cognitive legitimacy of news nerds, which is represented through recognition by external audiences such as the press and through achievements and recognition of news nerds with prestigious awards.

At the end of this chapter, I once again turn to the data set from the case study to systematically investigate the relationship between legitimacy and news nerds. Analyses are conducted at both the level of the professional (actor) and at the level of the organization. Together, the evidence at both levels of analysis further supports the role of legitimacy in the institutional augmentation of the journalism profession for news nerds.

Moral Legitimacy

Moral legitimacy is the integration of something new within the reigning, predominant standards; this is also sometimes referred to as normative alignment. Within the profession of journalism and the case of news nerds, this type of normative alignment would be evident, for example, in the integration of news nerd–related skills training within long-standing journalism education programs. This echoes one of the main claims in *Comparing Media Systems*—a seminal book on international comparative media systems by scholars Daniel C. Hallin and Paolo Mancini—that highlights the influence of the development of the journalistic profession on the media ecosystem.[5] There is indeed an interactive relationship in that educational programs both reflect journalism's professional standards and influence its culture.[6]

As discussed in Chapter 2, Northwestern University created a program merging journalism and computer programming in 2008. Columbia University launched a master's degree program in computer science and journalism in 2011 and created the Lede Program in 2014, which is a partnership between the Graduate School of Journalism and the Department of Computer Science that offers training in data and data technologies within the context of journalism.[7] The University of North Carolina at Chapel Hill also began offering journalist-developer courses in 2014.[8]

The University of Missouri has partnered with Investigative Reporters and Editors, Inc. (IRE) to run the National Institute for Computer-Assisted Reporting (NICAR) since 1993. Students, such as news nerd Ben Welsh who is currently the editor of the Data and Graphics Department at the *Los Angeles Times*, could and continue to be able to enroll in computer-assisted reporting (CAR) courses taught by the same instructors that teach professional journalists. Welsh describes his experience as a grad student at the University of Missouri's School of Journalism:

> That was where I just got to spend some time like learning how to code for real and doing dinky stories, and, in some ways, I was kind of there at, well, not, not a pivot point, but during a transition period in which

the CAR world is really changing from this investigative folklore sort of campfire, hand me down tradition of which Mizzou was one of the rare institutional things that like taught you how to do it right—and it was transitioning into this more digital, news nerd, web-like thing which you know to be honest didn't really exist before.[9]

The rise of moral legitimacy of news nerds is furthered by some of the technological developments discussed in Chapter 2 that served as disruptions to the news industry at large. As news nerd Alvin Chang explains, "as accessibility to technology increases and barriers to entry decrease very quickly, you can scrape a website. You can make a chart like *Snow Fall* and tech becomes more accessible to non-tech people." Chang, former senior graphics reporter at Vox Media and current senior data reporter at *The Guardian*, refers to the integration of tools that allow you to build things as "digital Legos":

> They're easier to incorporate into journalism classes because it's all about learning how to use this new technology—a school for learning how to learn. The challenging part is how to use the tools for journalistic ends. That's the direction we're moving in. All of the tools exist, but [now we are figuring out] what is the organizing principle behind how we use them.[10]

Of course, these are the examples of those first movers in the institutionalization of news nerds in academia—early indicators of moral legitimacy. As one news nerd explains, educational training does serve as an indicator of normative legitimacy especially with regards to hiring:

> We did have a few hires that didn't quite check that box [with regards to a journalism education], which was frustrating. The thing that happened over the course of the past few years is that there are a few programs that are addressing it, like the New School has a very interesting journalism design program, and they're putting out people who are learning how to code, learn how to design, think visually, but also learning about journalism, and they have some of the best minds in the data journalism and data visualization world teaching there.[11]

Indeed, since 2011, many more programs across the globe have started to incorporate news nerd–related training into their educational programs. In a 2016 survey of the 113 journalism schools accredited by the Accrediting Council on Education in Journalism and Mass Communications (ACEJMC), then PhD student and current Professor Charles Berret and his coauthor, lecturer Cheryl

Phillips, found that more than half of the schools (59 out of 113) offered one or more data journalism courses and 69 of the schools integrate some data journalism into other reporting or writing courses. The authors use "data journalism" to represent the "journalistic purpose of finding and telling stories in the public interest" in the form of data analysis, text, visualization, or news apps and through the use of computation, algorithms, and machine learning.[12] In 2018, Professor Bahareh Heravi at the School of Information and Communication Studies at University College Dublin put together an extensive data set that found 219 unique courses and programs on news nerd–related topics across the globe from programs fully centered on data journalism (e.g., at Cardiff University and University College Dublin) to classes focused on interactives and coding (e.g., Texas State University and City University of New York).[13]

Interestingly, the Poynter Institute for Media Studies conducted a survey of news educators and news professionals in 2014 and found that 80% of educators responded that the ability to tell stories with design and visuals was a very important skill for the future of journalism, while only 52% of professionals said the same.[14] This balance of intellectual and civic goals with the demands of the news industry has long been a challenge for journalism schools; technological disruption and associated new ways of consuming news has further exacerbated the imperative.[15] In 2015, the Knight Foundation published a report on the state of journalism education that concluded just that, "currency—the capacity to identify and master emerging market trends and media technologies and to integrate them quickly into journalistic work—is as critical to credible journalism education as command of Associated Press style and the inverted pyramid [were]."[16] It is worth noting that as one of the few credibility indicators of the journalism profession, the 2017 *Associated Press Stylebook* received $400,000 from the Knight Foundation to create a set of standards and spread the use of data journalism,[17] serving as another indicator of the moral legitimacy of news nerds.

Pragmatic Legitimacy

As important as normative alignment and cultural acceptance are for the legitimacy of something new, the economics have to work out as well. Pragmatic legitimacy is grounded in self-interest and functional superiority.[18] This type of legitimacy involves the linking of something new with actual economic outcomes.[19] The pragmatic legitimacy of news nerds is thus established through their connection with and impact on audience traffic, engagement, and business returns.

Even early on, those involved as news nerds affirmed the potential of this new form of the journalism profession. According to Jeremy Bowers in 2011, who at the time was a developer at *The Washington Post* and is now currently the organization's director of engineering, "data-driven news applications generate traffic and engagement. And as organizations continue to prove, they're also noteworthy pieces of important journalism."[20] Traffic success was demonstrated by the work of data journalist Nate Silver, who's site FiveThirtyEight was responsible for 20% of all *The New York Times'* traffic when he left to bring it to ESPN in 2014.[21] (FiveThirtyEight now sits under the purview of sister property ABC News, of which it and ESPN both fall under parent organization, the Walt Disney Company.) In 2016, the news applications team at ProPublica made up only about 20% of the newsroom staff, but their projects generated about half of the company's online audience traffic.[22]

As news nerd Ben Welsh explains:

> I bet you if you could get them to give you the numbers, you would see that the *New York Times* graphics department is—per person— the most profitable and most read section of the entire newspaper. I bet you, it's more than the politics coverage . . . I would bet that their COVID tracking stuff is probably the most read thing in the history of *The New York Times* by like some multiple . . . This is the change that's happening when you're suddenly the moneymaker.[23]

Even compared to other forms of important justification or legitimacy, it's pragmatic legitimacy that pulls news nerds into core organizational processes and into the newsroom. Welsh continues:

> You know, when I started 13 years ago, it was like "oh, there are some guys on the web who want to do some data thing," and the justification for that—which comes from the CAR tradition—is that it's for investigative reporting, which is a public service, and "we love the constitution, and we have some polls of readers that say they like investigative reporting." And sometimes they win a Pulitzer Prize and that's the justification for it. And I'm all for that justification—100% for it. But, when you're able to say like they can at the *New York Times* that "no, we're the most profitable. No, we have driven more subscriptions than anyone—AND, in an industry that's in crisis—that's game changer . . . That's where you get out of CAR and you get out of the projects, and you get into the main line business.[24]

The reality is that due in part to developments in technology and consumption behaviors, there are a variety of new ways to tell stories and when visual, interactive, and data elements are used in the right way and for the right story, engagement is high and business returns are good explains news nerd Julia Wolfe. "News organizations are seeing this as worthy investment, not just because of the great journalism—of which there's a ton—but also just from a business perspective," added Wolf, senior editor of data visualization at FiveThirtyEight.[25] News nerd Madi Alexander, data journalist at Bloomberg, agrees: "We get good readership numbers because we're creating exclusive content essentially, and you can't just Google and find the same story somewhere else."[26]

To illustrate, Wolfe offers *The Wall Street Journal* as one example of a news organization leading the way in news nerd legitimacy. She explains:

> There are a lot of different, great ways to tell stories and because of the decline in the medium of print, we now have opportunities to tell them very differently. For example, it's as simple as if you're working on a story on changing demographics in different countries, you can now really show what that looks like and what that means. And we find really high engagement on these things. When used in the right way for the right story, you can see good business return on [news nerds]. *The Wall Street Journal* is interested in growing subscribers and memberships and [news nerds] helps with that. There are numbers.[27]

As Tyler Fisher, former ProPublica and NPR news nerd, explains: "Vox Media is now using their product expertise as an actual revenue driver by selling Chorus. *The Washington Post* is also doing that of course." The current deputy director of technology at News Catalyst, which is a project based at Temple University that helps news organizations become sustainable in the digital media environment, goes on to say that as you look around, you can start to see news organizations that are really starting to figure out the economic benefits of news nerds and the pragmatic legitimacy of their work. Of course, he adds, "it really depends where you look."[28]

The pragmatic legitimacy of news nerds, however, has been a slow uptake. According to news nerd Ben Welsh, there has been a real, albeit gradual, sea change in the integration of news nerds throughout newsrooms, "The graphic staff is no longer operating as a support team to make simple charts . . . instead, it's focused on creating top stories of their own,"[29] but pragmatic legitimacy is just as slow to follow. On October 15, 2020, Walsh noted that three of the first four stories in the *New York Times* app were data driven, with the lead one— which included customized, tailored charts—bylined independently by a graphics reporter. According to Welsh, while these highly visual pieces are much more difficult and costly to produce, they are also "much more likely to resonate with readers, creating grand slam successes the old model never could."[30] Welsh explains:

> Shifting from the traditional model to the new model requires funda-mental reorganization and significant upskilling . . . I can only speculate, but if what we see at the *Los Angeles Times* holds true, I would predict that *The New York Times* graphics staff is putting up some of biggest readership numbers at the company. If that's right, there are likely strong economic forces that will encourage this trend to continue, at least at the news organizations with the leadership to make the change and the money to fund it.[31]

This is certainly a big shift in the institutional change process for news nerds, especially within the pragmatic legitimacy stage. "When I started in this field," writes Welsh, "the chief justifications for it were: A). Analysis that powered deep dive investigations; B). Web development for boutique internet experi-mentation. Now that graphics hit homers, this week, Kat Downs, the architect of a change like the one I'm describing was named a managing editor at The Washington Post."[32]

Hiring of news nerds—especially into top management positions—and human capital in general are also important manifestations of pragmatic legiti-macy and indications of the lengths that news nerds still have to go on their path to full pragmatic legitimacy. According to Alexander, time and money are still the biggest barriers to legitimacy and full institutionalization of news nerds through-out the journalism profession.[33] Having the right people is an especially impor-tant dimension for smaller news organizations that don't have the resources for mentoring or access to the supply of bigger market news organizations when trying to be successful with regards to the integration of news nerds.[34]

According to news nerd Sisi Wei, who at the time of interviewing was the deputy editor of News Applications at ProPublica and is now the director of programs at OpenNews, this is due to two reasons: financial resources and chal-lenges with supply. As she explains:

> I think every news organization would love to have [a news nerd]. I think there is a scarcity—a supply problem—and also a financial barrier. I don't think there are enough people who have these skills to work everywhere, like it's not so common in the sense that every small town probably has a journalist. I don't think the skills are so common that this is literally possible. Also, because it's not so evenly distributed, right, so the really big places have dozens of people. But the other thing

too is that there is a financial barrier. With these skills, you cost more as an employee and you're competing—not directly, in that sense that people who do this in journalism, I'm pretty sure, don't expect to make the same as they would in software—but, you cannot pay them the same amount that you would pay someone who has these skills in journalism. And so, I think there's a financial barrier there, and places have to make the investment.[35]

There is indeed a significant lag in the diffusion of news nerds particularly at smaller local news organizations where budget, infrastructure, and culture constrain integration of or even experimentation with new forms of professional journalists. Indeed, throughout my interviews with professional news nerds, news organizations' lack of the right resources was often mentioned as a barrier to further news nerd diffusion. News nerd Rachel Schallom, a project manager at *The Wall Street Journal* at the time of interviewing, explains that having the right people is an especially important factor in a news organization's success with regards to news nerds, and it is too often the smaller news organizations that don't have the resources for mentoring or access to the supply of bigger market news organizations.[36] An anonymous news nerd adds that success is "very dependent on the individuals" and that the most successful teams would fail to sustain themselves if those key individuals ever left.

Cognitive Legitimacy

Finally, in conjunction with both moral legitimacy and pragmatic legitimacy, comes an increase in public—or external—knowledge and awareness that signifies cognitive legitimacy.[37] Cognitive legitimacy is generally understood through the observations and assessments of those external to a profession itself, such as through media coverage[38] or prestigious award allocations.[39] In the case of news nerds, cognitive legitimacy is evident, for example, through the increase in media coverage of news nerds and the prestigious awards won by their work.

PRESS COVERAGE AS AN INDICATOR OF COGNITIVE LEGITIMACY

In an effort to illustrate the cognitive legitimacy of news nerds, I first turn to the archival industry materials. Recall from Chapter 1 that this data set includes over 320 articles from leading news industry trade publications (and for a more

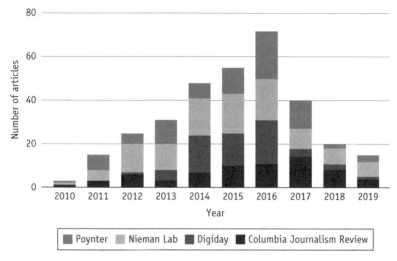

Figure 4.1 Press mentions related to news nerds, 2011–2019.

thorough explication of methodology behind this data set, please see the Data and Methods Appendix). Figure 4.1 illustrates the trajectory of trade press coverage of news nerds based on articles in this data set.

The trajectory is quite interesting and maps well onto expectations of the institutionalization path of something new, in this case, the development of news nerds as an augmentation of the journalism profession over the past decade (2010–2020). Between 2010 and 2016, the number of trade press articles mentioning news nerds increased steadily and starkly from 3 to 72 (a 2300% increase). In general, the number of trade press articles related to news nerds continued to grow each year between 2010 and 2016. The biggest change was from 2010 to 2011, when the number of trade press articles mentioning news nerds increased 400% and the smallest change was between 2014 and 2015 when the number of articles increased only 14.6%.

Between 2016 and 2019, the number of trade press articles mentioning news nerds steadily declined from 72 to 15, an 80% decrease. The decrease is certainly slower than the increase, averaging at about a 40% decrease each year. The biggest change was from 2017 to 2018 when the number of trade press articles mentioning news nerds decreased 50%.

As discussed, prior research has established that new forms that receive significant press coverage are likely to be perceived as legitimate, even when coverage is fleeting as it directs broader awareness to the given topic. In this way, press coverage of something new is often a precursor to diffusion or institutionalization as it filters out other potential competitors and guides public and industry attention to those seemingly with the most potential to survive rather than fail as a fleeting fad.[40] Sustained press coverage typically increases familiarity with a new form and educates relevant audiences about its functionality, which drives the birth rate of a new form.[41] Press coverage of an emerging professional form is expected to be an early indicator of cognitive legitimacy. As the above discussion illustrates, increased press coverage throughout the early part of the decade conferred legitimacy onto news nerds, contributing to their diffusion (to be discussed in Chapter 5) and the institutional augmentation of the journalism profession at large.

AWARDS AS AN INDICATOR OF COGNITIVE LEGITIMACY

While cognitive legitimacy can be indicated by press coverage in earlier stages of institutional change, cognitive legitimacy is also indicated by professional or industry-wide awards, which can be understood as "tournament rituals" that shape the configuration of organizational fields and thus impact institutional change.[42] When *The New York Times* received a Pulitzer Prize for its work on *Snow Fall* in 2013, for example, content created by contributions from news nerds was recognized in the award statement. This marked a turning point for the cognitive legitimacy of news nerds. As Schallom, currently the deputy editor of digital at Fortune Media, explains, "*Snow Fall* was a huge, interesting thing in the community because it got on the radar of so many traditional journalists that had no idea how we did our jobs. It won so many awards and other editors wanted that too."[43]

Furthermore, each year the Online News Association (ONA) holds the Online Journalism Awards (OJA) to recognize excellence in digital journalism. While OJA has existed since 2000, it wasn't until 2015 that news nerds were recognized with specific award categories. OJA introduced a new category dedicated to Excellence in Innovation in Visual Digital Storytelling that "honors exceptional and innovative efforts in telling stories through visual means: photos, graphics, illustrations, video, virtual reality or other emerging media."[44] Two years later, OJA introduced another new award category, dedicated to Excellence in Immersive Storytelling, which "honors exceptional efforts in telling stories through digital, immersive media: virtual reality, augmented reality, mixed reality, 360 video and other emerging media."[45]

Together, both traditional awards, such as the Pulitzer Prize and the Society for News Design's "Best in Show," and more modern, digital incarnations, such as OJA, have moved to include and recognize news nerds. This form of cognitive legitimacy is crucial for news nerds in their path toward institutionalization. As ProPublica news nerd Scott Klein wrote about his own news applications team, "we bring home prestigious journalism awards."[46] Indeed, several news nerds echoed the importance of getting their names on prestigious awards that serve as a valuable currency.

As one anonymous news nerd described while discussing those news organizations leading the way in news nerds: "If you go back and look at what they are doing in these newsrooms, they're winning huge awards. They're doing really important work that couldn't be done with traditional storytelling techniques." This news nerd then goes on to explain how following *The New York Times'* awarding of the Pulitzer for news nerd–driven work on *Snow Fall*, the company reorganized their newsroom to elevate "visual journalists and data conversant teams . . . You look around the landscape, and you see this making a big difference in the future of the field."[47] Together these events certainly served as one turning point in the institutionalization path of news nerds as an augmentation of the profession of journalism.

And so, a subsequent task of this chapter is to provide evidence concerning the role of cognitive legitimacy of news nerds over time with specific regard to their output and as recognized by industry awards. To accomplish this task, I chose to focus on two different award competitions from the Pulitzer Prize and the OJA and collected data on the winners. It should be noted, as Professor James T. Hamilton caveats in his stellar tome on investigative journalism, *Democracy's Detectives*, that journalism award winners are in and of themselves outliers by definition and using them to make a generalization about the state of journalism can be misleading. However, following his suit, the analysis of "prize-worthy material over time can provide insights into the journalism being held up as exemplary in a particular period"[48] and it certainly sheds light on that work that is deemed legitimate.

Thus, I collected data from the Explanatory Reporting and Feature Writing categories in both the Pulitzer Prize awards and the OJA from 2010 through 2020. For the OJA, each category was further broken down into large, medium, and small newsroom subcategories. An examination of the works cited for these awards yields a sample of 90 works from 2010 to 2020. Figure 4.2 illustrates the trajectory in award citations for journalism that incorporated news nerd work based on the awards data set.

In examining the award citations for Pulitzer Prizes in Explanatory Reporting and Feature Writing over the last decade, one can see that while news nerd–related work received some recognition earlier in the decade, it has consistently won an award over the last four years. OJA tells a different story because these categories began in 2012, thus a majority if not all of the recipients have incorporated news nerd work. It is interesting to note that while the above chart is based on the actual product and award winner, we can also look to another indicator of cognitive legitimacy in this arena—the text accompanying the award from the award-granting organization. Within the history of Pulitzer Prize awards from 2010 to 2020, the discourse that accompanies the award for recipients mentions news nerd–related work in 2011, 2013, and 2018. For OJA, the award discourse mapped quite consistently onto the actual work product.

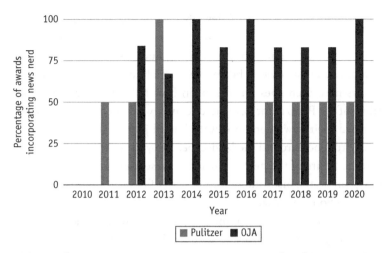

Figure 4.2 Award citations to projects incorporating news nerd work, 2011–2019.

Diving a bit deeper into the awards data set allows for some further insight into which news organizations are leading the way in news nerds—at least via the metric of producing award-winning news nerd journalism. Table 4.1 shows the list of exemplary news organizations producing award-winning news nerd work.

In the list of exemplary news organizations producing prizeworthy news nerd journalism, three organizations stand out. *The New York Times*, which accounts for over 13% of total award citations. And to a lesser extent, ProPublica and *The Seattle Times*, which each account for almost 7% of total award citations. Together, the top three news organizations generated 27.1% of the total awarded work.

Of course, part of this pattern relates to organizational size and resources. *The New York Times* is no doubt a leader in the journalism field with relatively ample resources to devote to new forms of the journalism profession. *The Seattle Times* and ProPublica, however, are certainly not in the same position. ProPublica is a nonprofit news organization, and as Hamilton explains in his book *All the News That's Fit to Sell*, *The Seattle Times* is a privately held company owned by the Blethen family, which does, however, have a history of willingness to invest in investigative reporting that leads to award citations.[49]

Case Study: Legitimacy of News Nerds at the Organization and Actor Levels

For a closer examination of legitimacy in action and what makes for a leading news nerd organization, we can once again turn to the case study of journalist

Table 4.1 **Distribution of journalism award citations for news nerd–related work across news organizations, 2010— 2020 (N = 59).**

News organization	Total no. of prize citations	Cumulative %
New York Times	8	13.6
ProPublica	4	20.3
Seattle Times	4	27.1
Arizona Republic/USA Today	2	30.5
Baltimore Sun	2	33.9
Boston Globe	2	37.3
Miami Herald	2	40.7
Mother Jones	2	44.1
New York Magazine	2	47.5
Washington Post	2	50.8
Outlets with 8 (N = 1)	8	13.6
Outlets with 4 (N = 2)	8	27.1
Outlets with 2 (N = 7)	14	50.8
Outlets with 1 (N = 29)	29	100.0

employment data. Analysis of the case study will also investigate the process in action at the actor level by analyzing what makes for a news nerd. The answers, as will follow, are based in legitimacy.

LEGITIMACY AT THE ORGANIZATIONAL LEVEL

With regards to the profession of journalism, legitimacy of news nerds occurs at both the organizational and at the actor levels through alignment with journalist norms, industry economics, and increasing public attention. Analysis of these three legitimacy indicators not only illustrates the role of legitimacy in the institutional augmentation of the journalism profession for news nerds, but it also provides insight into the characteristics that are thus associated with news nerd legitimacy. As such, another way to explore what makes for a leading news nerd organization is to examine which characteristics associated with legitimacy contribute to its position.

This question, however, requires a separate investigation from the previous case study analyses. Professors Nancy Leech, Karen Barrett, and George Morgan explain that a multiple linear regression[50] is the appropriate analytical tool when looking to predict a dependent variable from several other independent control variables.[51]

Organizational leadership in news nerds is measured with degree centrality in the news nerd network. Recall from Chapter 3 that journalist employment networks were generated from the employment data set to visualize the relationship between news organizations and news nerd jobs. This network was analyzed in an effort to better understand which organizations are leading in the hiring of news nerd jobs over time (see Figure 3.1 for the visualization). Degree centrality scores, which as you might recall from earlier chapters is the number of connections that an organization has with others in the network and can be used to indicate its popularity or importance in that network, were measured and recorded for each of the 15 sample news organizations within the network.

The five input variables are made up of two legitimacy indicators and three control variables. First, pragmatic legitimacy was measured as the number of news nerd positions under each organization in the case study employment data set. Recall that pragmatic legitimacy involves the linking of something new with economic approval or endorsement. In the case of news nerd, pragmatic legitimacy can be signaled through the dedication of resources to news nerd positions. For each organization, the number of news nerd positions was then divided by the total number of positions in the data set in an effort to normalize the measure.

Next, cognitive legitimacy was measured as the number of articles for each organization in the trade press data set. As we now know, press coverage is an indicator of organizational legitimacy[52] as it increases public knowledge and awareness.[53] As journalism scholars Thomas Hanitzsch and Tim Vos remind us, this is especially true for the news industry where authority, power, and control are derived from external perceptions of legitimacy.[54] Thus, I conducted a search for the total number of articles mentioning each of the sample news organizations in all four of the main publication sources (Columbia Journalism Review, Digiday, Nieman Lab, and Poynter). For each organization, the number of articles.

Finally, control variables included organizational age, size, and revenue. Founding dates for each organization were collected using information from the PrivCo database (for private organizations) and the MarketLine database (for public organizations).[55] Organizational size was measured by the number of journalists for each organization as listed in the CisionPoint database at the time of analysis. Utilizing information PrivCo and MarketLine again, annual revenues for each organization at the time of analysis were collected and recorded.

The multiple linear regression model assesses whether the independent legitimacy and control variables significantly predict the centrality of a news organization in the news nerd network (i.e., leadership in news nerds). When all variables are considered together, the answer is yes. Table 4.2 presents the results of the regression analysis.

This analysis tells us that the combination of pragmatic legitimacy, cognitive legitimacy, organizational revenue, age, and size significantly predicts central-ity in the news nerd network.[56] It also tells us, however, that pragmatic legiti-macy and cognitive legitimacy on each of their own is not a significant factor in determining if a news organization leads in news nerds. As we have learned, institutional theory sheds light on the importance of pragmatic and cognitive legitimacy for institutional change and in the case of profession of journalism, pragmatic legitimacy is indicated through the economic benefits of news nerds and cognitive legitimacy is indicated through external awareness of news nerds. While the role of pragmatic legitimacy and cognitive legitimacy were unsup-ported in the quantitative findings from this case study, the qualitative assess-ment conducted earlier in the chapter highlights the importance of these factors for news nerds at large.[57]

Interestingly, organizational age was the only independent factor to have a significant relationship with organizational centrality in the news nerd network. Furthermore, while institutional theory points to organizational age and size as inhibitors of institutional change, neither was found to be negatively significant.

Table 4.2 **Multiple linear regression for leading news nerd organizations.**

	Centrality in the News Nerd Employment Network
Revenue	−0.43 (0.00)
Cognitive legitimacy	−0.04 (0.24)
Pragmatic legitimacy	−0.32 (0.05)
Age	1.04* (0.00)
Size	−0.26 (0.00)

Note: Standardized coefficients reported. Standard errors are in paren-theses. * = $p < 0.05$
$R^2 = 0.48$; $F(5,9) = 3.54$.

In other words, an organization's size was not significant with regards to the likelihood that it would be a leader in the news nerd employment network. On a practical level, this indicates that the number of employees in a news organization has little bearing on whether it is an organizational leader in news nerds.

An organization's age, however, was found to be positively and significantly associated with leadership in the news nerd employment network. The significance of age can perhaps be explained by its relationship with organizational size and revenue. It is well known that older organizations tend to be larger organizations with more resources. This, coupled with the recognition that comes with older organizations, offers an advantage in hiring the necessary news nerds. Statistically speaking, the age variable may offset the size variable as the two measures conflate with one another to a certain extent. While older organizations may not ensure long-term leadership in news nerds, it is indeed a significant stopgap.

Furthermore, leadership in the news nerd employment network was measured with degree centrality, which makes the connection between age and leadership less surprising. Degree centrality was measured in the aggregate employment network in which central organizations with higher degree centrality scores are likely to be the established and entrenched players of the news industry with the resources necessary to hire news nerds. While established theory does indeed highlight the connection between organizational age and resistance to change,[58] more recent scholarship sheds light on the relationship between age and resources necessary for change,[59] which plays out as the case for news nerd and the journalist profession. On a practical level, this indicates that older organizations are more likely to be leaders in the news nerd network with regards to hiring trends and age may serve as an indicator of legitimacy.

LEGITIMACY AT THE ACTOR LEVEL

We can also use the case study of news nerd employment data to inform legitimacy and institutional change at the actor level and investigate the likelihood that a journalist is a news nerd from a combination of legitimacy and control variables. This analysis, too, requires us to turn to a new statistical application. Once again, we turn to professors Leech, Barrett, and Morgan who explain that a binomial logistic regression is the appropriate analytical tool for predicting a dichotomous and categorical outcome variable (e.g., news nerd or not) from a set of independent variables.[60]

The sample population consists of all current journalists in the employment history data set ($N = 3,587$ current journalists). Information from the employment data set was organized to reflect the educational degree (undergraduate major), graduate education (graduate degree), years as a professional (number of years since graduation), prior industry experience (industry of the job immediately preceding the current news job), diversity of prior industry experience (the number of unique industries in which each journalist had jobs), and the ratio of news nerd jobs to total jobs for each current journalist. On one level, these variables reflect the factors that interview participants (i.e., news nerds) suggest contribute to institutional change in the profession of journalism. In addition, they provide an opportunity to investigate the relationship among moral legitimacy, experience, and institutional change in the journalist profession. For further information on the methodology behind the data and analyses used in this section, please see the Appendix.

The binomial logistic regression model assesses whether the independent legitimacy and experience variables significantly predict whether a journalist is a news nerd. When all variables are considered together, the answer is yes. Table 4.3 presents the results of the regression analysis.

This analysis tells us that when all independent legitimacy and experience variables are considered together, they significantly predict whether a journalist is a news nerd.[61] It also tells us that the ratio of news nerd jobs to total jobs; prior industry experience in broadcast news, digital news, print news, or technology; and an undergraduate education in journalism, humanities, or visual and performing arts are each a significant predictor of the likelihood that a journalist is a news nerd. In other words, the odds of being of news nerd are greater for those with an undergraduate degree in journalism, humanities, or visual and performing arts. The odds also increase as the ratio of news nerd jobs to total jobs increases and when prior jobs are in broadcast, digital, or print news or technology.

This illustrates the importance of legitimacy—moral legitimacy, specifically— in action. Moral legitimacy, as measured with an educational degree in journalism (i.e., normative alignment), is a significant component of the model and thus has a positive relationship with news nerds and, specifically, the institutional augmentation of the profession of journalism for news nerds. Indeed, institutional theory sheds light on the importance of moral legitimacy for institutional change via normative alignment. In the case of the journalist profession, moral legitimacy is evident with the integration of news nerd–related courses into journalism education programs. Education plays a significant role in the likelihood that a journalist is a news nerd. Journalism education is impacting the positions that journalists take on once out in the industry. The emerging news nerd–related trends in journalism education (as discussed earlier in this chapter) and the significance of an undergraduate degree in journalism for predicting the likelihood that a journalist is a news nerd indicate that moral legitimacy plays both a practical and theoretical role in the institutional augmentation of the journalist profession.

Table 4.3 **Logistic regression predicting news nerds (N = 3,587).**

	B	SE	Odds ratio
Grad. ed.	−0.60	0.73	0.55
Grad. ed.—Journalism	0.09	0.86	1.10
Years in industry	0.01	0.02	1.01
Industry diversity	0.19	0.21	1.21
News nerd jobs / Total jobs	14.00**	1.00	3,240,978.58
Prior—Broadcast	3.23**	0.89	25.17
Prior—Digital	3.31**	0.94	27.29
Prior—Print	2.86**	0.90	17.45
Prior—Technology	2.65*	1.14	14.20
Prior—Entertainment	1.59	1.24	4.89
Prior—Publishing	2.08	1.17	7.98
Ed.—Journalism	1.99*	0.84	7.30
Ed.—Communication	0.00	1.03	1.00
Ed.—Business	−0.76	1.27	0.47
Ed.—Computer Science	−2.32	2.32	0.10
Ed.—Social Sciences	0.72	1.04	2.06
Ed.—Humanities	2.15*	0.88	8.62
Ed.—Natural Sciences	1.02	1.77	2.78
Ed.—Visual Arts	2.20*	0.99	9.03
Ed.—Engineering	−0.17	21.80	0.85
Ed.—Math	0.21	1.64	1.23

** $= p < 0.01$; * $= p < 0.05$.

Interestingly, while undergraduate education in journalism was a significant predictor of the likelihood that a journalist is a news nerd, graduate education was not a significant predictor of the same. It is possible that this is a result of the limited choice and lack of variance in journalism programming at the graduate school level or the insignificance of graduate school as a moral legitimacy indicator in general. According to the employment histories data set, only 16% of news nerds have a graduate degree in journalism and just 27% of news nerds have any graduate degree at all, while 31% of news nerds have an undergraduate degree in journalism.[62] On a practical level, these findings reinforce broader industry data on the percentage of journalists with undergraduate and graduate degrees in journalism. According to journalism professors Lars Willnat and David Weaver, 37% of U.S. journalists had a bachelor's degree in journalism in 2013;[63] just 9% of U.S. journalists had a graduate degree in journalism in 2002 (which is the most recent year with available data).[64] Undergraduate education in journalism is simply more prominent and thus more impactful. Indeed, change in news nerd education is leading at the undergraduate level.

Further findings indicate that an undergraduate degree in humanities or visual and performing arts are also significant predictors of the likelihood that a journalist was a news nerd. Many of the degrees categorized as humanities were for creative writing and many of the degrees categorized as visual and performing arts were for film. Intuitively, courses in both of these majors would touch on aspects of the news industry and/or journalistic norms necessary for practical success, which further supports the role of education as an indicator of moral legitimacy in the institutional augmentation process. In practice, journalists are significantly more likely to be news nerds with the moral legitimacy that comes from formal undergraduate training in journalism and associated course topics.

While theory expects early institutional change to be driven from outside the industry (recall Chapter 2), institutional change is expected to be driven from inside the industry as the process progresses. The statistical analysis outlined here indicates that in practical terms, these theoretical ideas hold true in the case study of institutional augmentation in the journalist profession. Indeed, as the process progressed, current journalists are significantly more likely to be news nerds if their prior job was within the news industry. Prior industry experience in print news, broadcast news, and digital news were all found to be significant predictors of the likelihood that a journalist is a news nerd. On the one hand, this finding reflects an institutional tendency to reinforce existing norms of the news industry. On the other hand, however, this also indicates a dearth of new blood—fresh perspective and experience that could, potentially, foster further change. Either way, this finding reinforces Shoemaker and Vos's call to attend to past experiences and established routines during times of institutional change.[65]

The significance of prior experience in the news industry is further supported with the significance of the ratio of news nerd jobs to total jobs. In both practical and theoretical terms, this indicates that news nerds remain news nerd and are less likely to become non–news nerds. This finding further reinforces the process of institutional augmentation as news nerds are not simply a fleeting fad.

Interestingly, prior experience in technology was also found—albeit to a lesser extent—to be a significant factor in contributing to the likelihood that a journalist was a news nerd. This finding is reflective of the institutional change process and the importance of those early outside entrants for institutional change in the profession. As change continues to occur, however, it is increasingly driven from within the industry and to a lesser extent from the technology industry. This indicates that in both practical and theoretical terms, prior experience from outside the industry—specifically in the related industry of technology—does play a role in the institutional augmentation of the journalist profession. The importance of experience outside the news industry echoes other recent findings on change in professions. Scholars Daniel Kreiss and Adam Saffer found that organizations comprised of individuals from diverse work backgrounds are more innovative.[66] At the actor level, this is similarly reflective of Craig Crossland and his colleagues who ascertain that diversity in career histories influences the likelihood that a CEO will lead a firm through change.[67]

Taken together, these results illustrate the importance of legitimacy in action at the actor level. Specifically, moral legitimacy (as manifested through an undergraduate degree in journalism) and prior experience in the news industry are significantly associated with the likelihood that a journalist is a news nerd. In practical and theoretical terms, the results of this analysis highlight the roles that education and prior employment experience play in the institutional augmentation of the profession of journalism for news nerds.

Summary

This chapter demonstrates the importance of legitimacy in the institutional augmentation of journalism for news nerds. Through interviews with journalists, qualitative analysis of industry documents and award citations, and quantitative statistical analysis of the case study employment data set, we can see evidence of news nerd moral legitimacy, pragmatic legitimacy, and cognitive legitimacy. In the moral vein, legitimacy of news nerds occurs via normative alignment, such as through the creation of news nerd–related journalism education programs. Pragmatically, legitimacy of news nerds is evident through the acknowledgment of the relationship between news nerd production output and financial benefits to news organizations. Cognitive legitimacy of news nerds is represented in the achievements and recognition of news nerds with prestigious awards.

This chapter argues that news nerds are legitimate and fully recognized throughout the journalist profession. "We're in a space that we weren't in five or six years ago. Everyone knows what it [news nerd] is," said one anonymous news nerd.[68] As Wei adds, "Most if not all news organizations understand that these [news nerds] are possible, even if they don't have one."[69] As these quotes illustrate, news nerds are legitimate throughout the profession of journalism; however, that does not mean that they are fully diffused. Wei goes on to explain that the community continues to grow but that not every news organization has a news nerd. They couldn't—there aren't enough of them. Indeed, from an organizational hiring perspective, "[news nerds] can fall from incredibly necessary to 'no, we need other skills first'" said one anonymous news nerd.[70] The diffusion of news nerds is thus the subject of Chapter 5.

5

Diffusion of News Nerds

News nerd Rachel Schallom describes her entrée into the profession of journalism in 2012 as "an interesting time to get in" as news nerd teams were just starting to get popular:

> It was right before *Snow Fall* was published. Work was getting done—
> especially at the higher levels, but it wasn't respected in the way that it
> is now. For a lot of us, when we were starting out, especially in smaller
> newsrooms, we were the only people in our newsroom doing this work,
> and so, the community was really important because that was really
> the only way that we could troubleshoot our code, or bounce ideas off
> each other, or continue growing to figure out how we could best do
> this work.[1]

Schallom, who was a project manager at *The Wall Street Journal* at the time of
interviewing, explains that a lot of news nerd work also introduced conflict and
challenges that traditional reporters didn't typically have:

> You know, we had to talk to IT departments about servers and what do
> we do when code doesn't work in our CMS [content management sys-
> tem]. There was a lot of figuring that stuff out because when companies
> bought CMSs and developed newsrooms, they weren't thinking about
> this type of [news nerd] work. So, it was a structural and organizational
> problem, as well as you know, we just need to figure out how to do this
> type of storytelling.[2]

The challenges associated with the new knowledge and skill sets of news
nerds within the profession of journalism, however, were met with an increasingly specific, objective, and diffuse community. According to Schallom, who is
currently the deputy editor of digital at Fortune Media, the community of news

News Nerds. Allie Kosterich, Oxford University Press. © Oxford University Press 2022.
DOI: 10.1093/oso/9780197500354.003.0006

nerds grew incredibly, and its accepting nature is one of the elements that fosters continued growth:

> The community atmosphere is something I would not have expected in journalism because journalism is highly competitive and the competitiveness is one of the things that I love about it—breaking news, beating people to the story, exclusives—all of that. But this community is so open. They'll send you the code and there is so much that is open source. There is a slack channel with people talking 24/7 about different ways of doing things. And when I was the only coder at the *Sun Sentinel*, that was a huge resource to me. I remember, there was this one interactive visualization that I was working on, and I could not figure it out. I broke the code, and I didn't know why. I ended up reaching out to a guy at *The Oregonian* who had done something really similar. And he ended up fixing my code, himself, and sent it back to me and then explained—in a 10-paragraph email—so that I would know how to do it in the future. And that sort of giving each other time is one of the most indicative things about the community—it happens all over the place. The community, I think, is really the reason why smaller and midsize newsrooms can succeed in this. Because the bigger teams are sharing their code, they are sharing their best practices, and we're not all starting from zero. So, this has really allowed the industry—and this part of the industry, specifically, to grow fast.[3]

So, while, Chapter 4 set out to explore the legitimization of news nerds, this chapter is all about the community of news nerds—the specification, objectification, and diffusion of news nerds throughout the profession of journalism. Chapter 4 utilized a variety of data sources and analyses that illustrate how the legitimacy of news nerds came about morally through normative alignment in educational training and organizational norms, pragmatically through the economic benefits tied to news nerd work, and cognitively through press coverage and award citations of news nerd work. Within a process of institutional change, however, legitimization is typically followed by diffusion, during which something new is compellingly justified as a potential solution to a specified challenge, objectified as increasingly established, and eventually diffused throughout a field.

As such, in this chapter, I explore specification, justification, objectification, and diffusion of news nerds in four ways. I draw on examinations of 10 years of journalism job listings, the case study employment data set, the industry documents data set, and interviews with professional journalists. Analyses of these data allows us to see the following patterns: news nerds are often justified as a potential solution to the specified challenges associated with technological, economic, and social change. Objectification is established via the increasingly visible community of news nerds in the form of professional organizations and conferences. And finally, demand for news nerds continues to follow suit as evident in the growing number of newsrooms with news nerd teams and the rising number of job listings hiring for news nerd positions.

Specification and Justification

For something new to be effectively diffused or widely adopted, it must first be explicitly justified as a solution for a particular, well-specified challenge. Within the profession of journalism, one way this occurred was through discussions of the connection between news nerds and overarching news industry challenges. Take, for example, *The New York Times*, which published an internal innovation report in 2014 (that was subsequently leaked to the public) emphasizing the veteran organization's struggle to compete in modern news. The shift toward news nerds—*the solution*—is framed as an imperative: "The only way to ensure that our report keeps pace is to build a newsroom with a deeper and broader mix of digital talents: technologists, user experience designers, product managers, data analysts, and most of all, digitally inclined reporters and editors."[4] The report continues:

> We want makers, who build tools to streamline our newsgathering; entrepreneurs who know what it takes to launch new digital efforts; reader advocates, who ensure that we are designing useful products that meet our subscribers' changing needs; and zeitgeist watchers, who have a sixth sense for the shifting technology and behavior. Most of all, we need those rare—and sought after—talents who can check off many of those boxes. And we need them now.

Furthermore, news nerds were justified as a solution to *the problem*—the challenges related to economics, disruption, and new entrants (i.e., digital-native news organizations), and technological and associated consumption behavioral changes (i.e., audience development). The most successful content—the innovations that readers found most engaging—was not being appropriately reflected by journalist talent and newsroom processes. As the report states:

> The surprising popularity of The [New York] Times dialect quiz—the most popular piece of content in the paper's history, with more than 21 million pages views—prompted weeks of internal discussions about

ways to build on that remarkable success. But over at BuzzFeed, they were busy perfecting a template so they could pump out quiz after quiz after quiz.[5]

Competitive digital-native news organizations, however, did not need to worry about new or retrained professional journalists. Instead, "[*The New York Times'*] competitors, particularly digital-native ones, treat platform innovation as a core function. Vox and First Look Media have lured talent with the pitch that they have built the tools and templates to elevate journalists."[6]

Specification and justification of news nerds at *The New York Times* was even more explicit several years later in a memo released by Executive Editor Dean Baquet and Managing Editor Joe Kahn that accompanied the newsroom's 2017 innovation report, "The Report of the 2020 Group."[7] In this memo, the editors specify that "the broader mobile landscape is increasingly a visual one—think of Snapchat, Instagram, YouTube—and we know that our mobile audience wants Times journalism to incorporate visuals even more fully into work." The editors present a four-pronged solution:

> We will hire significantly more visual journalists, as well as a small number of tool builders. We will train many, many more reporters and back fielders to think visually and incorporate visual elements into their stories. We will deploy new tools, such as Oak, a major improvement to our CMS, to make it easier for the newsroom to incorporate visual journalism in stories. We are changing the siloed nature of the newsroom when it comes to visual journalism.[8]

In essence, this memo formalizes news nerds as a new form of professional journalists at *The New York Times*. This is just one example of specification and justification—albeit an example at arguably the industry's leading news organization. Indeed, according to one reference to the report, "I doubt there is a newsroom in the world that wouldn't benefit from understanding the cultural issues laid out."[9]

Similar efforts occurred at other organizations as well. At *The Washington Post*, news nerds were hired to fill newly created roles of operations editor, product editor, and project editor. The formation of these positions was explicitly justified as a solution for producing quality and efficient content. As *The Washington Post* PR memo explains, these roles were created to help the news organization reach a wider organization, integrate new tools into the newsroom, and produce story projects "of the highest quality and built in a timely manner."[10]

Specification and justification of news nerds also occurred at digital-native news organizations such as FiveThirtyEight. According to founder and

Editor-in-Chief Nate Silver, the mission of the news organization is "defined by *how* we cover the news rather than *what* we cover," which is through data journalism and the associated professional journalists who, for example, apply statistics, visualization, and interactive development to news reporting.[11] These remarks accompanied the re-launch of FiveThirtyEight, which was part of *The New York Times* until 2014 when it was bought by ESPN. At the time, the remarks were widely considered to be a manifesto as they go on to call attention to the problems associated with news industry practices at large.[12]

Together, these examples are illustrations of how news nerds were justified as solutions to specified problems within the broader news industry. Change is portrayed as inevitable and the boundaries of journalism are fluid and flexible, accommodating new forms of professional journalists. Specification and justification suggest further normative alignment as represented, for example, through the idea that change is necessary in order to meet the economic realities and the changing needs of consumers.

Objectification

Objectification plays an important role in the diffusion stage as well, especially within the context of journalism. Here, objectification is established via the increasingly visible community of news nerds as a new form in the profession of journalism. Annual conferences such as National Institute for Computer-Assisted Reporting (NICAR), Online News Association (ONA), and SRCCON (discussed more thoroughly in Chapter 3), as well as Hacks/Hackers Meetups, and even a Slack channel called News Nerdery each contribute to an objective community for news nerds.

News nerd Rachel Schallom highlights the role of SRCCON specifically, which is the conference run by OpenNews that began in 2011. She explains that it "was the first conference dedicated to people who code in newsrooms, or people who work with people who code in newsrooms, so it's like data and code—specific. And that really gave us a community and validated the work that we do in newsrooms."[13]

According to one anonymous news nerd, NICAR specifically attracts both journalists who have been working since the earliest databases trying to gain respect in the newsroom *and* emerging advanced programmer journalists who love working on data and design—a mix that contributes to an open and supportive community. This news nerd goes on to explain:

> I've been going to [NICAR for the] past few years, and at that conference, you find more established investigative journalist and data

journalists who have been working for years—you know people who have just been doing this since the earliest databases and fighting the newsroom trying to show how important it was to be able to do statistical analysis on stuff when they were probably the only people conversant in data in the newsroom back in the eighties. And then you also have this huge mix of young people who are programmers who are like very advanced programmers and are passionate about working with data and have some design sensibilities. That to me is like, wow this is great! It's such an open, supportive community.

Together, NICAR, Hacks/Hackers meetups, the News Nerdery Slack channel are all spaces for an objective community of news nerds to come together and they "embody this exciting new frontier within journalism."[14]

Schallom shares similar sentiments and explains how crucial the community is for the existence of news nerds:

No one paid attention to us in newsrooms, and you know you weren't considered part of the core team. That has definitely changed over the last five years. But I think this community was so necessary for these people that were doing the work in the early days because they just wanted someone to talk to, you know about their work . . . And the community, I think is really the reason why smaller and mid-sized newsrooms can succeed in this because the bigger teams are sharing their code; they're sharing their best practices. And we're not all starting from zero. So, it's really allowed the industry, and this part of the industry to grow.[15]

Diffusion

Indeed, objectification of news nerds is established via the increasingly visible community of news nerds—especially in the form of professional organizations and conferences. And as such, demand for news nerds continues to follow suit through diffusion—a stage of institutional change during which news organizations increasingly hire news nerds or launch news nerd departments and teams. In a report by writer and digital governance expert Alexander B. Howard, data journalism was "mainstream" as early as 2014; the market for data journalists was "booming" at an estimated thousand across U.S. newsrooms and continuing to grow given the demand from both traditional and digital native news organizations ranging from *The New York Times* and *The Economist* to FiveThirtyEight and Vox.[16] While data journalist is just one of many of the various titles representing news nerds, Howard, who is currently the director of the Digital Democracy Project at the Demand Progress Educational Fund, goes on to qualify his assessment by explaining that "the number of people applying data science to journalism or practicing high-level computational journalism" is much smaller, with the top talent "split between the New York Times, ProPublica, NPR, the Washington Post, the Chicago Tribune, the Wall Street Journal, and the Los Angeles Times."[17]

For further evidence, we can now return to the case study employment data set for a more granular analysis of the development and diffusion of news nerds. Figure 5.1 summarizes the general change in the number of news nerd jobs in the employment data set. Each line represents the growth of news nerds within a different sector of the news industry: broadcast news, newspapers, and digital-native news. Numbers are reflective of new news nerd jobs as a percentage of new journalist jobs each year. The results highlight the growing prominence of news nerd jobs across this period of analysis.

During the period from 2011 to 2015, journalist jobs changed both across each news sector and within the news nerd category. According to the employment data set of the case study, 1,086 new journalist jobs emerged in broadcast news, newspapers, and digital-native news in 2011; 16 were news nerd jobs. The number of news nerd job openings grew, reaching 40 out of 1,387 new news jobs in 2013 and reaching 105 new news nerd jobs out of 1,845 new news jobs by 2015. In general, it is clear that there has been a significant upward trend with regards to the presence of news nerd–related jobs within the newsroom. Indeed, even by 2015, news nerds were a small but important part of contemporary journalism.

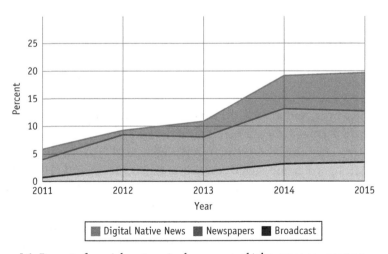

Figure 5.1 Percent of new jobs categorized as news nerd jobs across news sectors.

The development of news nerd jobs is more nuanced when examining each news sector individually. In 2011, there were 5 new news nerd jobs out of 664 new broadcast news jobs (<1%). By 2015, there were 31 new news nerd jobs out of 899 new broadcast news jobs (4%). As for print news, there were 7 new news nerd jobs out of 218 new jobs overall in 2011 (3%). By 2015, there were 33 new news nerd jobs out of 356 new print news jobs (9%). Interestingly, while the number of new news nerd jobs continued to increase in print news, there was a decrease in the number of overall print news jobs, further reinforcing the prominence of news nerds. In digital native news, there were 4 new news nerd jobs out of 201 new jobs in 2011 (2%). By 2015, there were 41 new news nerd jobs out of 590 new digital-native news jobs (7%).

While the general pattern of news nerd job development looks quite similar in both print news and digital-native news sectors, it is comparatively much more stable in the broadcast news sector. News nerd jobs have grown substantially in print and digital-native news sectors, accounting for an estimated 6% of all new jobs in those sectors. In broadcast news, news nerd jobs account for an estimated 2% of all new jobs.

News nerd employment has indeed increased in both print news and digital native news sectors, accounting for an estimated 6% of all jobs in those organizations. Furthermore, as the number of new news nerd jobs in print news continued to increase over time, the number of new journalist jobs in print news overall continued to decrease. This is in line with general news industry trends as jobs at traditional news organizations continue to decrease and further reinforces the finding of an increasing ratio of news nerd jobs to total jobs.

Further insights are gained when comparing traditional news (print and broadcast sectors) to digital native news. In 2011, new news nerd jobs as a percentage of total new journalist jobs were generally the same in traditional news and digital native news. In 2012 and 2013, traditional news organizations hired more news nerd workers as a percentage of total new journalists than digital-native news organizations. This changed by 2015 when new news nerd jobs as a percentage of total new jobs was higher in digital-native news than traditional news.

The increasing importance of news nerd positions is further apparent when examining the specific nature of the jobs. In 2011, there were only 16 new news nerd jobs listed in news organizations. The majority of these roles are social media associates and social media coordinators. In 2015, there were 73 new news nerd roles listed. These jobs evenly reflected social media, data, development, and programming; over half of the job titles include reference to editor, journalist, or reporter (e.g., data journalist and news applications editor). This reflects a clear shift toward the integration of news nerd jobs within the newsroom.

DIFFUSION OF NEWS NERDS AT THE
ORGANIZATIONAL LEVEL

Indeed, as writer and senior scholar of the Poynter Institute for Media Studies Roy Peter Clark explains, the ultimate diffusion of news nerds at a variety of news organizations would reflect the merging of skills and values on behalf of the reader.[18] In addition to an examination of diffusion across the industry, however, it is prudent to explore the process at the organizational level as well. Recall from Chapter 3, the anecdote about *The New York Times*' 2013 *Snow Fall* story, perhaps the most famous example of early integration of news nerds and their work in a Pulitzer Prize winning piece. In 2013 alone, more than 100 *Snow Fall* imitations sprung up from newsrooms of various sizes and geographical locations. This illustrative news nerd work was so diffuse that Alexis Sobel Fritts, then an editor at Columbia Journalism Review, pointed to the sparking of a new word: "Snowfalling (*v., to funnel all one's resources into a single digital story*)."[19]

Snowfalling is illustrative of mimetic isomorphism, which is a central tenet of institutional theory used to explain how organizations model the successes of others within the industry in order to conform to expectations and enhance legitimacy.[20] Mimetic isomorphism typically occurs in uncertain and rapidly changing contexts and is often decoupled from pragmatics and internal efficiency demands.[21] As such, it can be used to explain the early adoption of news nerd news by organizations that might not have had appropriate resources, which would further the process of diffusion.

In addition to the numerous examples already discussed about news organizations hiring news nerds or launching news nerd teams, there are plentiful more illustrations of diffusion across a variety of news organizations. At digital-native news organizations, other examples of news nerd diffusion include BuzzFeed's News App team in 2014 and Vox's data journalism team. Exemplifying diffusion at more traditional news organizations, the Associated Press formed an interactive news technology team in 2013 tasked with creating data-driven, interactive, and platform-focused news content. The team is comprised of journalists with significant technical skills (e.g., data visualization and web development) as well as investigation and story development skills—a combination that differentiates news nerds from other developers. According to Team Editor Troy Thibodeaux, the team represents a shift away from the "model in which visualization or interactive storytelling is an afterthought, an illustration of the story, and toward a model in which this work is central to developing the story and enables us to tell the story in ways impossible for straight text reporting."[22]

In a 2018 memo on the decade anniversary of ProPublica, Editors Stephen Engelberg and Robin Fields, along with President Richard Tofel explicitly discussed the diffusion of news nerds over the course of the newsroom's history. They wrote:

> Our use of data analysis and visual storytelling has expanded substantially. The initial staff of ProPublica included just two people who knew how to write computer code and could put our stories on the web and create, when needed, a graphic or two. In the years that followed, we've added a team of data journalists and news application developers, as well as web designers and producers.[23]

Sisi Wei, who at the time of interviewing was the deputy editor of ProPublica News Applications, explains her team as a combination of developers and data journalists:

> Everybody on the team is a journalist responsible for their own reporting if they're doing a project, but on top of that, they are the news app developers, and are also responsible for doing interactive graphics or any searchable database or public service tools that we might build for our journalism. So that for us means doing a combination of data journalism as well as design and programming in order to create your final work whether that's a piece or a visual storytelling element or something that's like a searchable database online. It can sort of come out in many different ways, but that's what half of the team does, and the other half are data journalists who do heavy data analysis and data bulletproofing and trying to make sure everything we do is up to standards when it comes to data science. And so, my job as deputy editor is to essentially help edit both visually and in content.[24]

Wei is now the director of programs at OpenNews, but since her tenure, news nerds at ProPublica have continued to diffuse. In discussing the impact of news nerd diffusion at ProPublica, the memo adds:

> We've taken on some of the most sophisticated statistical work ever attempted by journalists, exposing the racial biases in an algorithm meant to help judges forecast future criminality and comparing individual surgeons' complication rates. We've harnessed large data sets to empower consumers, creating features like Dollars for Docs, which has been used nearly 20 million times to look up payments doctors received from pharmaceutical companies . . . We've built immersive interactives like "Hell and High Water," a collaboration with the Texas Tribune, which presciently showed the perils Houston, America's fourth-largest

city, could face from a major hurricane—almost a year and a half before Hurricane Harvey hit.[25]

News nerds are diffusing to smaller and regional news organizations as well. At the *Los Angeles Times*, Ben Welsh runs the Data Desk, which is a team of journalists and programmers tasked with data collection, organization, analysis, and visualization. At the Minneapolis *Star Tribune*, CJ Sinner is the digital graphics producer tasked with data analysis and development of interactive charts and graphics within the newsroom. At *The Oregonian*, the Data-Driven Enterprise Team is responsible for data journalism and the creation of data-driven applications, interactives, and visualizations.

As news nerd Jeremy Bowers, director of engineering at *The Washington Post*, explains:

> My general feeling is that this is all just sort of pushing forward relatively quickly. It feels like the big change came in maybe 2013, 2014 when it felt like a lot of folks who I was talking to at various newsrooms were adopting this real product-focused mindset that was close to a way that a standard tech company would do business, which I thought was pretty intriguing. ProPublica was doing it at that point, Texas Tribune, Marshall Project—these are small investigative news outlets and in the case of the [Texas] Tribune, policy shops. But if you look at their engineering teams, they are basically run like a standard engineering organization that happens to have a very good newsroom attached to it.[26]

The integration of these news nerd teams within newsrooms of varying sizes and geographical locations is indeed indicative of real diffusion and transformation. As former ProPublica and NPR news nerd Tyler Fisher explains, "in 2014, the best news nerd teams were off building their own apps and not driving the product as a whole." Recall pioneer news nerd Brian Boyer who worked at NPR in those days, and, according to Fisher, "apps.npr.org was a totally separate server"; it was not impacting the main product. "That's starting to change as news nerds are more and more integrated within the newsroom as a whole."[27]

According to Aron Pilhofer, who at the time was the associate managing editor for digital strategy at *The New York Times* and is now a professor of journalism innovation at Temple University, these are indeed not teams comprised of the traditional skills of newsrooms from pre-2011.[28] The strength of this community embodies a new frontier for journalism, which is increasingly comprised of people with coding, designing, and journalism backgrounds coming together to tell new and exciting stories. In fact, according to a report released by the

Tow-Knight Center for Entrepreneurial Journalism at the CUNY Graduate School of Journalism and former NPR executives Mark Stencel and Kim Perry, there is a big market for journalists with experience and expertise in code, visual storytelling, and audience analytics.[29]

In fact, to gain a better sense of this market and the change in journalist job positions, we can turn to the data set of journalism job listings. Job listings are textual representations of industry labor markets and especially useful as indicators of change.[30] In the context of the news industry, for example, journalism scholar Brian L. Massey used them to understand the demand for multiplatform reporters in 2010,[31] and scholars Sally Young and Andrea Carson used them to understand how news organizations themselves defined "journalism" during a particularly transformative year for the industry (2009–2010).[32]

The journalism job listings data set used here provides seven years of data (2010–2016) and includes approximately 8,000 listings of journalism job openings.[33] Each listing includes a time stamp, job title, employer, and job description. The listings were also further coded to reflect traditional journalist versus news nerd positions according to the established coding scheme utilized on the employment histories and verified by professional journalists. Figure 5.2 illustrates the rise in job listings for news nerds as a percentage of total job listings within the journalism job listings data set.

During the period from 2011 to 2016, job listings for journalists changed considerably. According to the job listings data set, there were 981 listings for journalist positions in 2011 and only 12 of these listings were for news nerd positions. In general, the majority of these 12 positions were reflective of traditional computer-assisted reporting (CAR) and/or data-journalist positions such as this job listing for a database editor at *The Wall Street Journal*:

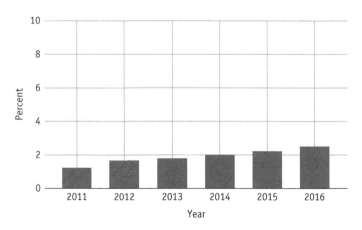

Figure 5.2 News nerd job listings as a percentage of total job listings.

We're seeking an entrepreneurial, creative journalist to launch a broad-based data-mining initiative. Our ideal candidate is a methodical reporter with a strong background in database research and reporting, with a keen eye for spotting trends and a talent for working across many subject areas and bureaus. Candidates should have experience in working with reporters, shaping coverage and teaming with disparate groups to create value for our readers—and also be prepared to roll up their sleeves to help produce online pages and work on strategy for the Web section.

By 2013, however, the number of news nerd job listings more than doubled to 28 news nerd job listings out of 1,539 journalist job listings. There were 30 news nerd job listings out of 1,181 journalist job listings by 2016. Notably, even as the total number of journalist job listings declined, there was an increase in news nerd job listings.

To illustrate the evolution of news nerd job listings, consider this 2016 listing for an interactive news developer at *The New York Times*:

The Interactive News desk at The New York Times is looking for creative, interdisciplinary thinkers with strong technical backgrounds . . . Interactive News is the special digital projects team embedded within the newsroom of The New York Times. You'll be working with editors, reporters, photographers, designers and other developers to create newsroom-facing tools and reader-facing projects that expand the horizons of our digital news report. Our department's goal is to practice web development and software engineering as a newsroom craft. We draw on technical expertise to imagine new editorial forms. Most of our work is published in collaboration with other newsroom departments. Your role is to bring digital creativity and software expertise . . . No journalism experience is required.

This job listing is clear about the integration of web development and software engineering expertise and responsibility within the newsroom. Notably, explicit journalism experience is not a requirement; however, the right candidate is expected to be involved with news production and distribution.

More and more, news nerds are diffusing throughout the journalism profession. Indeed, Fisher says, "if you look around the industry, you can see places—often the more successful places—have started to figure this out." Fisher, currently the deputy director of technology at News Catalyst, which is a project based at Temple University that helps news organizations become sustainable in the digital media environment, goes on to add that as the fiscal situation for journalism grows more and more dire, news organizations will increasingly see the successes of these more prominent news organization in utilizing news nerds and try to learn from them.[34]

Barriers to Complete Diffusion

Together, these developments, statements, and activities suggest that news nerds are generally diffusing throughout the profession of journalism. Of course, not all news organizations have fully embraced news nerds in their newsrooms—nor are all able to even if they so desired. Concerns abound regarding the replicability of news nerd work and the practicality of news nerds throughout the industry, especially at local and regional organizations that might not have the labor and resources to incorporate it. According to Pilhofer in 2014, "The 400+ journalists at NICAR still represent something of an outlier in the industry, and that has to change if journalism is going to remain relevant in an information-based culture."[35]

News nerd Sarah Slobin, who was the "things editor" at Quartz during the time of interviewing, expands on this imperative and explains that as the news audience continues to shift to mobile and the gap between long- and short-form content widens, "news organizations that put their own legacy systems ahead of catering to how we read on the internet will continue to have to make difficult decisions and those that can deliver short, customized new experiences that cater to readers will continue to grow."[36] Slobin, currently a visual editor at Reuters, foresees print news and magazines moving to more of a "bespoke, keep-sake" application; whereas good reading experiences with strong journalism that is well presented will have more of a "long tail" as long as it is delivered in a way that is "shareable, savable, and comes with a good user experience." The bottom line is that successful news organizations must incorporate news nerds and their work in order to remain relevant in addressing audience demands.

Emily Bell, founding director of the Tow Center for Digital Journalism at Columbia Journalism School, finds a similarly slow but encouraging shift in that "what was once a hostility by journalists toward 'the techies' has become an admiration and understanding that journalists with the right technical skills hold the keys to the survival and health of the field."[37] Indeed, as is often the case with something new, especially in the context of the history of the journalism profession, news nerds were initially met with hostility and resentment from legacy newsrooms and legacy news workers. Fisher explains that it was common for newsrooms not to know what to do with news nerds. He says, "things have changed in fits and starts, but I still hear the same, 'I don't get respect for my work' or 'I don't have a real role in my newsroom.' "[38] In fact, according to research and writer Zara Rahman, the common thread among news organizations with successfully integrated and diffused news nerds is actually "an acknowledgment at all levels within the newsroom that technical literacy and technical skills can open the door to new forms of storytelling."[39]

In that way, the enablers of and barriers to diffusion of news nerds throughout the profession of journalism exists at the organizational level; however, it exists at the more micro, actor level as well. Simply put, many legacy journalists aren't interested in learning the unique skill sets that make for a news nerd. As news nerd Alvin Chang explains:

> A good way to think about it is how labor economists think about people who are unemployed who are highly skilled but older: so, because they are highly skilled and have a lot of job experience, they don't want to learn new skill sets—and why should they? They don't know if it will pay off. That's pretty apparent once you get to people of a certain experience level. The more accomplished and experienced someone is at having been in the journalist profession without having had a strong quantitative edge, the more resistant they are to the "here's a new skill set."[40]

Erin Medley, who was the director of editorial and audience development at New Jersey Advanced Media at the time of interviewing, notes a similar resistance from legacy journalists but adds that she has seen a bit of a shift as well:

> There's definitely been an evolution because, I mean, because there just had to be. At a certain point, you can't push back on everything and so you learn to embrace it, it has been slow going. Some people, you know, learn quicker than others and some people are more cut back than others, and I think that with the infusion of new staff members, people coming in who have more of a [news nerd] background than the traditional journalists, there is a realization of "oh, I have to touch up, this is the way forward." I actually saw a T-shirt the other day that had a slogan that perfectly sums up the newsroom transition from print to digital, and it said, "Don't look back, you're not going that way," and I really think that that should go up in every newsroom. It's like stop saying, "well, back in the day, we did this" or "back when, you know, we were still using typewriters," and it's just like we get it. Of course, there are definitely things that should be valued from the past in that newsroom experience like integrity and accuracy in your reporting and exposing crimes and other things in society that the public should

know about. For sure, we should look back on that. However, looking back on when you were using a typewriter is probably not the thing to focus on—those are the things that you can let go.[41]

Chang, former senior graphics report at Vox Media and current senior data reporter at *The Guardian*, goes on to argue that this type of actor-driven resistance is only one facet of the barriers to news nerd diffusion throughout the profession of journalism while the other is that the profession simply doesn't have the right approach:

> You don't go into journalism because you love math, which is fine. But you also don't go into journalism because you love the scientific method (which is also fine). However, all of these things need to contribute to the ways that we analyze and evaluate our news. Our news judgment is based on some subjective, pie in the sky thing where we are like, "yes, that's news judgment, this is good news judgment or bad news judgment." But the kind of thinking that brings that about is more cultural than it is a quantitative approach to something or an objective, scientific approach to something. The more that we can encourage that type of thinking, the better off.[42]

However, even within newsrooms that have embraced news nerds, struggles persist, especially with regards to alignment with organizational structure and culture. As an anonymous news nerd explains, "To integrate these things successfully, you have to figure out newsroom culture and fit . . . figuring out where these skills have the most impact in terms of daily work process of journalism wherever you are is critical."[43] News nerd Brittany Mayes, graphics reporter at *The Washington Post*, echoes this sentiment:

> At the end of the day, it takes a very intentional effort to integrate our daily work into what the rest of the newsroom considers the work of a journalist. I don't know what that looks like, but if we are seen as others, it's not going to happen. We won't be able to advance. Journalism is a little popularity contest—a who's visible contest. Until we are recognized, we will be stuck in a category that isn't considered above the fold content.[44]

The problem is that news organizations are historically "bad at self-improvement and learning new skills—to their detriment," said news nerd Brian Boyer, who was the head of Product Operations at Spirited Media at the time of interviewing.[45] News nerd Julia Wolfe, senior editor of data visualization at FiveThirtyEight, adds that news organizations that treat news nerds with the same respect, expectations, and responsibilities of traditional journalists "see the greatest output . . . the newsrooms that are integrating [news nerds] into the newsroom are excellent."[46]

As news nerds continue to develop as an augmentation of the journalism profession, job titles and expectations are still inconsistent, which perhaps limits the extent to which thorough diffusion and eventual institutionalization can occur. According to one anonymous news nerd, there currently are no agreed-upon professional standards; those coming into news nerd roles have varied backgrounds and complicated work histories ranging from computer science and biology to journalism and design. This news nerd finds that they are often treated as "the mistress" at legacy news organizations, and while things have definitely improved over time and it varies by organization, it is "still decades off from being settled into what this means and from having the legitimacy that it deserves."[47]

Echoing this sentiment, news nerd Mayes adds: "We are going to have to be recognized as more than news nerds. We are still trying to figure out where we fit in the newsroom and that's why having an identity for the community is so important."[48] Another anonymous news nerd agrees that it is an "interesting" and "weird" moment right now but adds that it is "hopefully settling down a little bit more to where it will just be like, 'Oh you're a journalist too, and you just use these different tools.' "[49]

Wolfe, however, has noticed substantial change with regards to job titles over the years as she explains that she had three different titles at each of her three jobs even though she generally had the same responsibilities. By her own account, she was a digital designer doing journalistic work and telling stories, but not under the purview of the newsroom in 2014. By 2015, Wolfe's job as a news app developer explicitly included the responsibilities and expectations of a traditional editor and, specifically, a byline on all news output. She explains:

> It was really the first newsroom I was in where I did kind of feel like, you know with some exceptions, but for the most part, treated like a reporter with a lot of the same expectations of quality news judgment, careful editing, and that I would help, not just say "how do we make this pretty," but "how do we tell this story best."[50]

The evolution of job titles is echoed in news nerd Rachel Schallom's—as mentioned, current deputy editor of digital at Fortune Media and former project manager at *The Wall Street Journal* during the time of interviewing—description of her own experience, which she cites as an "amazing" transition over the past five years.[51] According to Schallom, news nerds are finally core members of the newsroom, although there are of course still struggles to ensure their opinions are as valued as traditional journalists. "We're still fighting the good fight for equality, but I think we're getting closer and closer to where teams are or are more integrated in newsrooms and are less seen as service desks," which is more of an acknowledgment that news nerd skills are a necessary integration in all aspects of a newsroom.

This shift in how news nerd teams are viewed within a newsroom was frequently mentioned in interviews when discussing the barriers to diffusion of news nerds throughout the journalism profession. Echoing Schallom's sentiment, news nerd Brittany Mayes explained that "one thing that is perpetually a question is about our work is how to not be considered a help desk, and that is still not solved."[52] Mayes, a graphics reporter at *The Washington Post*, describes her personal experience with this barrier as progress is slowly made in how colleagues within the newsroom view news nerds. Earlier in her career, Mayes noted that her non–news nerd colleagues in the newsroom assumed she could do work in a matter of minutes or hours, and she once overhead a colleague describe her team as those who "work with journalists to add data to a story." Mayes was shocked, "Yikes. We're not even the journalist in this situation."

Moving forward, especially in an effort toward institutional change within the profession at large, news nerds and their work must be viewed as valuable. According to Mayes, the tides are slowly changing as traditional journalists increasingly work with news nerds and become more accustomed to collaboration, while those higher up in the editorial organization see real value in news nerd work. "Once newsrooms start prioritizing the work that we're doing with similar standards of a journalist who focuses on words as opposed to visuals, then a lot can change."[53]

The Current State of the Diffusion of News Nerd Throughout the Profession of Journalism

In 2016, OpenNews, which as you can recall from Chapter 2 is a network of developers, designers, journalists, and editors working at the intersection of journalism and technology that launched in 2011, set out to better understand the news nerd community with a News Nerd survey that received responses from 514 journalism-focused developers.[54] According to the publicly accessible results, 44% of respondents have been working in "journalism tech" for more than four years, while this was the first "journalism tech" job for 14% of respondents. Almost three-quarters of the respondents (71%) work at news organizations.[55]

The survey organizers note that job title was a question of particular interest to the community.[56] More than 50% of respondents have a title of news app or interactive developer, and 33% of respondents chose "other" (there were a total of 11 additional built-in choices). This lack of consensus is an oft-mentioned challenge of institutional change and perhaps reflects the development stage of news nerds as a new form of professional journalists.

One year later, OpenNews—in partnership with Google News Lab—expanded the survey to 756 respondents (more than a 47% increase) at the intersection of journalism and technology.[57] Here again, the goal of the survey was to better understand who news nerds are, how they learn and support one another, and where they go next. Of the respondents, 55.6% of news nerds had been working in journalism-tech for five or more years, and 69% of respondents work on what's categorized as "journalism" (e.g., stories, data journalism, news applications, graphics); other responses, for reference, include mobile apps, the news organization's core website, or the news organization's CMS.

Interestingly, the top three reported job titles were reporter (about 17.8%), developer (16.2%), and editor (16.1%) compared to something more specific like graphics editor (6.4%) or data reporter/journalist (3.3%). These results are staggeringly different than one year prior when only 3% of news nerds had a job title of reporter and 8% had a title of editor. In a sense, the shift toward incorporating news nerd skill sets and responsibilities into the institutionalized profession of "reporter" or "editor" as opposed to qualifying the role as "graphics editor" or "data reporter" is an indication of reinstitutionalization wherein the new thing replaces the old as the taken-for-granted form of the profession. While this trajectory of objectification and diffusion is merely one small facet of an institutional change process, it is certainly worth noting. Will every professional reporter and editor be expected to incorporate news nerd skills into core journalistic processes? Or is there space in the profession for reporters that do and reporters that don't? These questions and more will be attended to in the following chapter on institutional augmentation.

Summary

In sum, this chapter demonstrates the processes of specification, justification, objectification, and diffusion of news nerds throughout the profession of journalism. Through a variety of data sources ranging from job listings to employment data, to industry documents, to professional journalists themselves, we can start to see the relatively diffuse state of news nerds. It is clear, however, that news nerds are not fully diffused throughout the profession of journalism or the news industry at large. So, what does that mean for the process of institutional change and the future of the journalist profession? It is precisely these questions that I seek to address in the next and final chapter.

6

Institutional Augmentation and the Future of News Nerds

For the longest time, the nerds, as I will affectionately refer to them, these folks were working on the internet which was like the bastard cousin of the thing that we produce, so in my case it was newspapers but in others', TV or radio. The website was very much a second-class citizen. I mean, here at the *Post*, the website was literally a different company. It was across the river for years. It was called the Washington Post Newsweek Interactive. You could work with relative impunity, but you didn't really have a career ahead of you. You weren't advancing in any meaningful way. You certainly weren't making changes to the way the broader organization was reporting or editing or chasing stories or building products. And there are still holdouts. But I feel like especially in the bigger places and smaller places—the holdouts are mostly in the middle—the folks who are nerdy have caught up. They're in positions to be agenda setting.[1]

The above quote from news nerd Jeremy Bowers, director of engineering at *The Washington Post*, captures the institutional change of news nerds within the profession of journalism. Over the last decade plus, early change was reflective of the entrance of outsiders from technology and science industries bringing new news nerd–related knowledge and expertise to the news industry. Newsrooms slowly started to experiment with news nerds, but it was done in a very ad hoc basis as illustrated with Bowers's anecdote in which *The Washington Post* news nerd team was a different company, a "second-class citizen . . . across the river."

As the decade progressed, pragmatic legitimacy through the financial effects on a news organization and cognitive legitimacy through the prestige of news nerds winning awards for their work helped propel the increasing diffusion of news nerds both within news organizations and across the news industry. These observations hint at an important yet infrequently discussed aspect of institutional change: What happens when the process differs from the traditional

News Nerds. Allie Kosterich, Oxford University Press. © Oxford University Press 2022.
DOI: 10.1093/oso/9780197500354.003.0007

binary options of reinstitutionalization or failure? The community of news nerds continues to grow and gain prominence, so much so that the profession of journalism has augmented for news nerds to coexist as a supplementary form of professional journalist.

The preceding chapters demonstrate that institutional change in the profession of journalism occurred with specific regard to the development of news nerds. Together, the quantitative and qualitative analyses offer clear evidence of the disruption and destabilization of established industry practices and the entrance of new players in the professional field. Experimentation and evaluation of something new (i.e., news nerds) within the confines of news organizations themselves followed. Morally, pragmatically, and cognitively, news nerds became legitimate both within the boundaries of the profession and outside of it, leading to increasing diffusion of news nerds throughout the news industry and the institutional augmentation of the profession for news nerds.

In this chapter, I thus consider this process of institutional augmentation and how it can be analyzed to address important questions on the future of news nerds and the news industry at large. Here, I address two main areas of questions raised by the case study of news nerds and the profession of journalism. First, what is the current status of news nerds within the profession of journalism, and why? In other words, are all journalists news nerds? Should they be? Furthermore, how has the empirical study of the institutional augmentation of news nerds served as an explanatory framework for change in both theoretical and practical contexts? Second, what are the implications of institutional augmentation and this collision of old routines of the profession of journalism with the new? In unpacking the implications of the case of news nerds on journalism and its role in society, I will also address next steps for news nerds as journalism begins to think about managing new positions, new competencies, and new ways of understanding.

Are News Nerds Journalists?

The institutional augmentation and the updating of the profession of journalism for news nerds differs from the traditional model of institutional change in a significant way. According to the extant literature, as explicated in Chapter 1, something new gains moral legitimacy during theorization, which fosters further adoption and pragmatic legitimacy during diffusion, and eventually becomes a cognitively legitimate arrangement that is reproduced unquestionably over time. Once a new structure or routine is fully institutionalized, it is expected to survive uncritically as the authoritative approach.[2] Indeed, institutional change in any context is a long-term process that results in a binary outcome: either reinstitutionalization, which would indicate the full institutionalization of something new as the taken-for-granted, natural, and appropriate arrangement or the failure of something new as a fleeting fad.[3]

The account of the process through which news nerds developed within the profession of journalism, however, is illustrated through a four-pronged explanatory framework: (1) precipitating jolts and deinstitutionalization, (2) experimentation and evaluation, (3) legitimization, and (4) diffusion that ends neither in reinstitutionalization nor failure. In other words, is every news nerd a journalist? Is every journalist a news nerd?

According to Bowers, news nerds in the newsroom should have newsroom titles. "Standardization is useful in a career. Steven Rich at [*The Washington*] *Post* is a wonderful reporter. Calling him a data reporter might add a note that he's different and nonstandard. That's not what you want to do."[4] News nerd Brittany Mayes, graphics reporter at *The Washington Post*, disagrees with the sentiment:

> On the one hand, it's limiting to put everyone under [the same] title just because they do nontraditional reporting. [On the other hand,] I don't think stripping us of "news nerds" and distributing us throughout the newsroom is the right way because we can't be under an editor that has no idea what we do. It would be more frustrating than being on a team together and having editorial staff above you that works in both capacities. But that does make us disconnected from the newsroom.[5]

In reality, there is a need to recognize the difference in skill sets and competencies at all levels of the news business. Former ProPublica and NPR news nerd Tyler Fisher offers that perhaps "it would help newsrooms at large to accept that we are reporters who just happen to write python, but I do think that the other side of argument is these are new skills that need to be recognized, understood, and emphasized." Fisher, currently the deputy director of technology at News Catalyst, which is a project based at Temple University that helps news organizations become sustainable in the digital media environment, adds that, in general, change doesn't succeed if you try to fit something new into an old structure. "It needs to be more fundamental. Change needs to happen at the product level and at the business level."[6]

Indeed, there are pragmatic legitimacy reasons for differentiating news nerds from the traditional profession of journalism. Ben Welsh, editor of the Data and Graphics Department at the *Los Angeles Times*, describes himself as "pro nerd, nerd positive." He explains that perhaps it's his "contrarian, outsider personality" that allows him to welcome being the "weird one," but while there are some who take the view that news nerds should be a part of the traditional journalist profession and branding them as different sets them outside of that, he does see some important benefits to such a stance:

> I think that being a nerd is a good thing. To be frank with you from a strictly economic point of view, especially if our departments are going to become successful and profitable, I think that people in our niche have been underpaid. I'll be totally honest with you, based on what they make and what you could make in the market with similar computer programming skills. And the case I make to my employees when they don't like me saying nerd all the time . . . is we need to be clear and upfront about the extra skills that we're bringing to the table here.[7]

As news nerd Alvin Chang tells it, the start of the 2010 decade brought with it the hiring of developers and designers, and the incorporating of technology skills into the newsroom. "It turned out, however, that it was hard to incorporate those tech-minded people into the newsroom." Chang, former senior graphics reporter at Vox Media and current senior data reporter at *The Guardian* argues that now that newsrooms have all of these tools to make a chart, or interactive, or app, there's a push in newsrooms to move away from the developers that built the tools to the reporters that can just use them:

> There's a self-consciousness when your title is just "reporter" or "editor," and you have these [news nerd] skills, but if you don't have that [news nerd reference] in your title, people assume that you don't have those abilities. That's why "graphic" is in my title. There is some separation that this person knows how to do something different.[8]

Chang does, however, see a decrease in the emphasis on differentiation as there are more and more reporters who know how to do programming tasks, for example. "There is a move toward occupational development. It's goal oriented. It's not about a shiny new toy, it's about goals." Indeed, news nerds and their augmentation within the profession of journalism are not a symptom of "shiny things syndrome," as academic and journalist Julie Posetti dubs the news industry's "obsessive pursuit of technology in the absence of clear and research-informed strategies," instead, they are a value-driven integration of something new to efficiently and effectively connect with audience demands.[9]

The journalistic value of efficiently and effectively connecting with audience demands through news nerds and their competencies will only continue to increase—even if it's gradually. This means, according to Welsh, that news nerds must accurately reflect what they do and the value that they bring to the table—especially younger news nerds:

I think that there are people my age who sometimes feel like, well, if I say I'm a programmer, then I'm not a journalist and that reflected a certain moment in time. As things get more integrated, I think it's more normal. I think we're just going to see more people who have programming skills in all professions. But I don't think that the majority will be [news nerds]. It's a specialization. It takes years to learn.[10]

Indeed, in the case of news nerds and the profession of journalism, neither reinstitutionalization nor failure occurred. In other words, any journalist can be a news nerd, but not every journalist should be a news nerd. The profession of journalism has augmented enough so that both can coexist without one displacing the other. News nerds augment the boundaries of the traditional, institutionalized profession of journalism, but they do not supplant the traditional journalist.[11]

INSTITUTIONAL AUGMENTATION

And so, in synthesizing this case study of news nerds and institutional change in the profession of journalism, I propose institutional augmentation as a useful explanatory framework for understanding the process and outcome of institutional change in both theoretical and practical contexts across a range of industries. Simply put, institutional augmentation represents institutional change that results in neither the displacement of an existing institution nor the failure of the new one. Instead, existing institutions are updated and augmented to allow for the coexistence of supplementary institutions. Institutional augmentation thus provides useful language for examining institutional change that results in stable diffusion without full institutionalization—an outcome that differs from the traditional binary options of institutionalization or failure. The process of institutional augmentation is illustrated in Figure 6.1.

The importance of institutional augmentation. Prior work on institutional change in journalism finds that oftentimes the symbolic relevance of something new is just as important as its economic relevance.[12] The notion of institutional augmentation provides language for describing a similar scenario. News nerds are fully theorized. Their symbolic relevance and legitimacy are pervasive throughout the industry; however, they are not fully diffused. Their economic relevance is realized to the extent that they have displaced traditional journalists. In other words, institutional change in the profession of journalism has resulted in an updating and augmentation of traditional journalists to allow for coexistence of news nerds.

Scholars have studied the process of institutional change across a variety of contexts, generating valuable insight into how and why the process occurs;

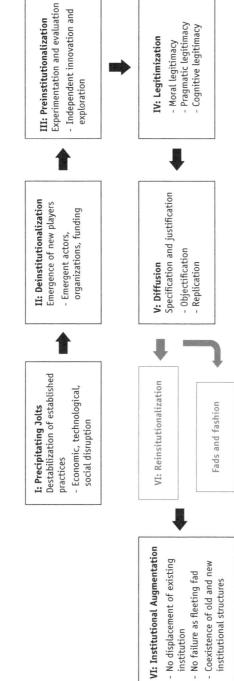

Figure 6.1 The process of institutional augmentation.

however, processes of institutional change resulting in neither institutionalization nor failure are not well understood.[13] Institutional augmentation serves as
an explanatory mechanism for alternative outcomes of change. Furthermore,
the case of the journalist profession suggests that institutional augmentation is a
useful explanatory mechanism of institutional change for other industries. Take,
for example, the case of transportation and the development of electric vehicles
or the case of television and the development of social analytics for measuring
audience consumption. Framing institutional change as institutional augmentation provides scholars and analysts with a basis for delineating outcomes that
allow for supplementary institutional structures.

The development of electric vehicles, for example, certainly began as an
attempt to displace gasoline vehicles. Ultimately, the new variant of the car
did not displace the existing variant of the car, nor did it fail as a fleeting fad;
instead, the two types of cars coexist as taken-for-granted vehicular transportation options. A similar outcome occurred in the television industry with the
development of social television analytics as a method for measuring the audience. Social television analytics did not displace traditional television ratings,
nor did it fail as a fleeting fad; here too, both institutional structures coexist as
taken-for-granted mechanisms for measuring audience consumption.[14] Indeed,
institutional augmentation helps account for this alternative in which institutional change results in augmentation of an existing institutional structure for
the coexistence of a new one.

Institutional augmentation in practice. In addition to the above theoretical discussions, the findings in this book also provide a number of practical
implications for both the news industry as well as for a wider variety of industries. With regards to the practice of news, the key findings in this book indicate
that institutional change in the journalist profession has indeed occurred: news
organizations increasingly integrate news nerds into the newsroom, and the
relevance and legitimacy of news nerds is pervasive throughout the industry;
however, news nerds are not fully diffused, nor have they displaced traditional
journalists. This is partly due to a lack of resources—both on the organizational
end and with regards to supply. Indeed, not every traditional journalist is a news
nerd. Instead, the profession of journalism has updated and augmented to allow
for the space and coexistence of news nerds.

Furthermore, the findings in this book also answer some important questions
about the mechanisms that drive institutional change in professional journalists.
Indeed, news industry practitioners can benefit from an understanding of the
potential alternative drivers and outcomes of institutional change. For example,
experience and education from within the news industry are found to increase
the odds significantly of a journalist being a news nerd. While some of the
early—and perhaps, more familiar—examples of news nerds are those coming

from outside the traditional experiences of journalists, this is not the case for the majority of current news nerds.

In some ways, those news nerds following an atypical news industry path are suggestive of "black swans," a term coined by finance scholar Nassim Nicholas Taleb and applied to the 2008 financial crisis.[15] A black swan describes an unpredictable occurrence that deviates from the norm and yet has significant implications. In the context of news nerds, some of the most prominent early news nerds are those who came from technology or science industries and arguably made significant impacts on the change process. The findings suggest, however, that this is not the typical case. News organization managers can thus benefit from investing in the training of journalists for news nerd positions.

The shift toward news nerd positions is of course not unique to the news industry. As discussed in the introductory chapter of this book, a variety of industries are impacted by the increased role and relevance of data, analytics, platforms, and products. Thus, the relevance of these findings on institutional change extends beyond the confines of the news industry. In general, the results of this research shed light on the different outcomes of institutional change and specifically in understanding when something new is real (as in, an institution), when it is a trend (as in, a failed fad), and when it is somewhere in the middle (as in the case of institutional augmentation). This knowledge has the potential to guide organizational decision-making regarding the investment of time and resources into new things, such as in the hiring of professionals. As such, this book also heeds recent calls from industry and academia to extend work to other fields in an effort to increase relevance and foster cross-discipline conversations.

Implications for News Nerds and Journalism: The Collision of Old and New

This book chronicles change in the profession of journalism to provide a nuanced understanding of its composition over a decade of time from 2011 through 2020. In doing so, it is quite clear that the makeup of the profession has changed with the increase in prominence and prevalence of news nerds. Building on prior literature in institutional change and journalism studies, I introduced the concept of institutional augmentation as an alternative framework for understanding the development of news nerds and the institutional change in a profession that results in neither the displacement of the old nor the fleeting of the new.

Indeed, institutional change occurred throughout the profession from the introduction of "cybergeeks in the newsroom" through the legitimization of news nerds both internal and external to the news industry.[16] The current stage of diffusion helps illuminate the viability of institutional augmentation and the potential for coexistence of both an existing (old) and a new institutional structure.

The book tells a story built from a combination of industry data and interviews with professional journalists to show how news nerds are quantitatively and qualitatively different from the traditional professional journalist. As is evident from this research, however, as institutional change progresses, these news nerds have not undergone full institutionalization to the point where they have displaced traditional journalists. Nor have they failed as a fleeting fad.

Instead, the institution of the journalism profession has updated and augmented to allow for the coexistence of both the old and new forms of professional journalists. This argument and the associated findings of the case of news nerds have profound implications for the role of journalism in society. They implore us to think about the processes necessary to sustain journalism and its ability to inform in contemporary society. With ongoing technological transformation, economic fluctuation, and changing social preferences comes the need for institutional augmentation in the profession of journalism and thus within news organizations themselves if they are to survive and thrive and continue (or, hopefully, improve) their role in informing society.

Indeed, the collision of old and new, specifically via the institutional augmentation of the profession of journalism for news nerds, illustrates key concerns for journalism's continued role in society. These concerns can be grouped into three overarching categories: organizational power structures, business literacy, and representation of diversifying audiences. First, as the case of news nerds shows us, journalism requires strategic change throughout the profession by disentangling and revamping power structures and career paths to emphasize access to data, code, and a general culture of experimentation. Second, journalism of the future must foster cultures of innovation and business literacy with an openness to new approaches and business models. And finally, the case of news nerds illustrates that for journalism to survive, it must find new ways to meet audience needs and new ways to represent the audience it serves. As news nerd Jeremy Bowers said to me, he is currently focused on what to do now that they're not "building an insurgency":

> You have all the tools at your disposal, but you also have things that you have to maintain. You have a great institution that you have to keep working with. So, how do you do your insurgency, but keep it informed by the values of your big company? That's where the future is to me.[17]

As such, in these concluding sections, I will examine just that—the implications of news nerds for journalism and its ability to inform in contemporary society. More specifically, I will address the implications of this study through a discussion on designing the next phase of the profession as new skill sets and new ways of understanding and producing news start to collide with the old routines of journalism, and what that means for journalism's role in society.

POWER STRUCTURES

Journalism scholar Wilson Lowrey found that as a subgroup, visual journalists were able to greatly influence newsroom norms but *only* when they were given authority.[18] Indeed, norms of varying subgroups can come into conflict especially when struggling for power and control. As the new and old collide, news nerds need real power in the newsroom. According to news nerds Brittany Mayes and Tyler Fisher, in their 2019 SRCCON panel on "designing the next phase for newsroom technologists," this would mean that news nerds need to sit at the top of the food chain—in editor and management positions, as well as in journalist positions in an effort to push forward a tech- and news nerd–focused mindset. Collaboration across desks is also fundamental to help those that aren't necessarily typically empowered by technology so that they don't see news nerds as workers with some magical skill set, but rather journalists with a discipline or a craft, like any other part of profession. Importantly, news content is shaped by these struggles,[19] and thus, attending to and understanding the power trajectory of news nerds is imperative. This understanding gives insight into how news work is changing, specifically through news nerds and their work, as a response of relevance to continued external change.

Indeed, diffusion of news nerds throughout newsrooms (which, of course, implies the hiring of news nerds throughout newsrooms) is a fundamental first step in fostering a culture of data, code, and experimentation. However, to sustain institutional augmentation throughout the profession, newsrooms need retention plans in addition to hiring plans. At a SRCCON panel in 2019, news nerds discussed several imperatives for news organizations in the management of news nerd career paths and the sustainability of their careers within the profession of journalism. First, it is important that news organizations minimize the competitive moments among news nerd employees by making sure not to pit news nerds against each other because of salaries and promotions; ideally, these processes should be transparent. One news nerd explained that the competitive nature was reflective of the field of journalism as a whole in that—perhaps, due to or at least made significantly more precipitous by the economic downturn—there are two clear tiers of employees in a news organization: full-time journalist and contractor journalist. According to this news nerd, competitive tiering hurts professional culture in a deep way, and it is indicative of how upper management thinks about its employees. One route to sustainability of news nerds as an augmentation of the profession of journalism is certainly to avoid this competitive nature through transparent hiring, salary, and promotion processes.

Second, news nerds also encouraged one another to leverage external resources in an effort to hold an organization accountable should processes go awry. There is no need to strictly rely on internal organizational mechanisms. Instead, there is a consensus on the utility of organizations such as OpenNews, Columbia Journalism Review, Nieman Lab, and other external voices who can shine a light on bad behavior in a way that would be consequential.

Third, and perhaps most vociferously required for the sustainability of news nerd careers within the profession of journalism, was transparency and demystification of the job (i.e., with regards to salaries, promotions, and the job role itself) and relatedly, management of career paths for news nerds. To specify, news nerds are looking for more agreement on titles and responsibilities for their job roles and career paths.

To whit, freelance journalist Masuma Ahuja wrote in an article for Poynter on her experience without a clear career path in news. She writes:

> For years at the beginning of my career, I was simply the internet kid. I began working in large, legacy newsrooms. At my first few jobs, my titles were fluid, my duties unspecific. I was defined, mostly, by the fact that I knew how to internet . . . But the fact that I was a digital person meant that my path was distinct from the reporters I worked with, sat near, and looked up to. Because I didn't want to write for print or produce for TV, the options available to me often sat at the intersection of strategy, editing and programming—finding ways to take existing journalism and put it in new places. But the thing I love doing best is reporting and telling stories. I often use the internet and technology to help me do this better, but the journalism remains at the heart of what I do.[20]

Interestingly, one of the questions in the OpenNews and Google News Lab survey of news nerds asked why news nerds left a job over the past five years, and the top reason was a lack of promotion or career pathway opportunity (20.3%).[21] Only 27.8% of survey respondents were news nerds in a management role with one or more direct employee reports (versus 67.3% of news nerds who are not in such a role).[22]

One paragon exception, of course, is *The New York Times*. Bowers recalls his previous stint at the *Times* and how Dean Baquet, executive editor, was smart but not necessarily news nerd savvy:

> He was really good at knowing what he did and didn't know. He appointed two people to his masthead who are A grade, number one, superstar news nerds: Matthew Ericson and Steve Duenes. They're both just absolute geniuses and really sharp. And he knew that he

needed full, masthead level positions to really help make sense of [news nerds] . . . It's a place that's kind of got their head on straight. Not only do they have these people [news nerds] working as deputy editors on various desks, but they also have masthead level roles for people who are data heavy or web savvy or however you characterize it. So, I guess that's kind of what the future looks like to me is that slowly but surely the folks who didn't grow up with the internet are going to phase out, they're going to retire, they're going to take other jobs, and there's going to be a new wave of folks for whom the internet is just a thing that they've always had.[23]

Indeed, news nerds are looking for better management of their careers. In particular, more promotion and hiring of people into top management positions who understand and work with technology would make for more effective and efficient leadership of news nerds. The OpenNews and Google News Lab survey also found that while many news nerds hoped to develop their technical abilities, they were also highly interested in building managerial skills and in bringing in project management support. When asked about the biggest challenge facing their news organizations in "developing or using technology as a core journalistic practice," 39% of respondents cited a lack of editors who are qualified to supervise technologists.[24]

This echoes media scholar George Sylvie who in his book, *Reshaping the News,* calls this pattern out as a typical one across the board (and, not just in the case of news nerds) and an imperative one that news organizations solve.[25] Sylvie explains that while editors are responsible for leading their assigned newsroom reporting departments, they aren't typically trained as leaders with the competencies necessary to make and manage change. As is most often the case, newsrooms promote their best *reporters* with high reporting competencies into open editor roles, and thus many editors must learn leadership competencies on the job. Oftentimes, the institutionalized routines of the profession of journalism make it resistant to change.[26]

As an augmentation of the profession of journalism, news nerds are characterized by the development of new skill sets and competencies within a newsroom, yet they also play an important role in driving cultural change. As Federica Cherubini, the head of leadership development at the Reuters Institute for the Study of Journalism, explains in a piece on the future of journalism, these types of roles will only continue to grow in importance as news companies increase their digital development and thus the news industry must be "thinking about how these roles—and the people in them—can evolve." She goes on to argue: "When you are creating a new role (and many of these are created by those who end up in them), it's difficult to know where you are going and what you're measuring yourself against."[27] Indeed, news organizations need to be thinking about career management for news nerds.

As journalism scholars Mark Deuze and Brian Steward argued in Deuze's (2011) edited volume on *Managing Media Work*, media management must be about the management of careers and not just about the management of companies.[28] This becomes even more imperative as media workers and media managers continue to move away from traditional, siloed roles and toward more flexible and overlapping skill sets,[29] such as in the case of news nerds. This implies that news organizations require a focus on and transparency about the career management of nontraditional journalists such as news nerds to sustain institutional augmentation throughout the profession of journalism at large, and thus continue to adapt to meet the changing demands of the news consumer in an attempt to sustain (or return to) prominence in the public sphere.

BUSINESS LITERACY

In her book on interactive journalism, scholar Nikki Usher found that as emergent actors, interactive journalists brought new ways of thinking and doing into the newsroom due in part to their varying backgrounds and perspectives.[30] As is discussed throughout this book, similar processes occur with news nerds as well—especially for early news nerds who come from outside the traditional bounds of the news industry to share their training and experiences with the profession of journalism. For all news nerds, however, there is a spirit of doing things in new ways—a spirit of experimentation and development that newsrooms need to foster to cultivate the next phase of institutional augmentation as old and new forms of the profession of journalism collide.

At a SRCCON meeting in 2019, one news nerd explained that it was a challenge to make innovation and experimentation priorities throughout the entire newsroom in that you could offer kits and tutorials on new equipment and processes to journalists but getting them to take the time away from their main job responsibilities of reporting and editing was difficult—especially if it took more than one or two tries. Oftentimes, change management within a news organization is focused on the end user (i.e., the audience) and not on the impact of change on internal processes. Including early *and* late adopters of innovation along the way throughout organizational processes is key. An understanding of the cost of innovation and an understanding of business literacy, however, are crucial to furthering the change process—to fostering the growth of news nerds, to advancing technology and storytelling, and to meeting the new demands of an ever-changing audience. Indeed, a culture of experimentation helps the news industry adapt to the changing methods by which readers now want to consume the news.

The Covid-19 pandemic, for example, is undoubtedly a story told in data, maps, models, and predictions—all of this the work of news nerds helping the public understand critical information about the health of their communities. Unfortunately, this pandemic will likely not be the last; the work of news nerds and the news nerds themselves are critical, as is the need for the business literacy that surrounds this need.

According to journalism scholars Alfred Hermida and Oscar Westlund, "the epistemology of data journalism has long held the promise of being a more accurate and reliable form of reporting, using social science methods to analyze quantitative data using computers."[31] The pandemic and continued social, political, and economic unrest often bring along increasing questions of trust in journalism. As is evident from the COVID-19 pandemic, journalism can indeed shape scientific innovation and public policy. News nerds rose to the challenge by acquiring, visualizing, and communicating vital data when the public needed accessible information. News nerds, in abiding by such a data epistemology, will continue to play a role in mitigating those questions with the credibility and relevancy that comes with advancing their practices. Managers will do so by cultivating the business literacy necessitated for doing so.

REPRESENTATION OF DIVERSIFYING AUDIENCES

Lastly, it's imperative to note that even if news nerds are empowered through organizational culture and career management, the community itself must address its own diversity and inclusion challenges. According to news nerds Brittany Mayes and Tyler Fisher, in their 2019 SRCCON aforementioned panel, this would mean that news organizations are representative and inclusive of the audiences and communities that they serve. Hiring—getting a diverse mix of people on the team—is paramount for listening to audiences and their needs, for centering audiences in storytelling.

Indeed, much of the profile of news nerds throughout this book focuses primarily on educational attainment and diversity as far as training and industry experience; however, there are of course other individual traits that presumably shape which types of people become news nerds (e.g., a gender dimension, a racial dimension, a class dimension).[32] As is the case with most social phenomena, the opportunity to be a news nerd is not randomly or equally distributed across the population.

We can refer to the OpenNews and Google News Lab survey of the news nerd community for some insight into who is a news nerd based on some of these dimensions. In 2017, 426 news nerds identified as male compared to 310 who identified as female. This made for a more balanced gender composition than the respondents of the community survey the prior year in which 252 news nerds identified as male and 117 identified as female. To put it differently, there was a 165% increase in the number of self-identifying females in the news nerd community from 2016 to 2017.[33]

As far as racial composition, roughly three-quarters of the news nerd community in 2017 identified as white, which is just about the same as the results from the prior year. In 2016, 13% of news nerd respondents identified as Asian as compared to 10.5% in 2017. In 2016, 6% of news nerd respondents identified as Latino as compared to 5.8% in 2017. Finally, 3% of news nerd respondents identified as Black in 2016 as compared to 3.7% in 2017.

When we analyze who is a news nerd, we see that there is certainly unequal gender and racial distribution. Indeed, when asked about what the news nerd community needs, 29% of respondents cited some variant of diversity.[34] As journalism continues to grapple with a diversity reckoning, the same applies for news nerds. In an effort to sustain institutional augmentation in the profession of journalism, news organizations must grapple with ways to evaluate and rethink their commitments to diversity and inclusion, as well as the representation of the audiences and communities that they serve.

In sum, as we use the case of news nerds to understand the process of institutional augmentation, we can see how the interaction of external forces such as the destabilization of established practices and the entrance of new players in conjunction with internal processes of experimentation and evaluation sets the stage for legitimization and diffusion of news nerds. These processes thus create a space for institutional change in which neither reinstitutionalization of news nerds as the new professional journalist nor their failure as a fleeting fad occurs. Instead, the profession of journalism is updated and augmented to allow for the supplementary existence of both of old and new.

It is with this collision of new skill sets and new ways of understanding and producing news with the old routines of journalism that the findings of the case of news nerds provide implications for the role of journalism in society by imploring us to think about processes necessary to sustain journalism and its ability to inform in contemporary society. With ongoing technological transformation, economic fluctuation, and changing social preferences comes the need for institutional augmentation in the profession of journalism and thus within news organizations themselves. In the case of news nerds, this means more than emphasis on the latest technology. It means strategic change throughout the whole of news organizations via an emphasis on power structures, cultures of innovation and business literacy, career management for nontraditional skill sets, and diversity, equity, and inclusion as the news industry continues to grapple with the challenges of our digital society.

Appendix: Data and Methods

The following appendix material outlines my methodological approach to assessing a process of institutional change, specifically focusing on the case of the profession of journalism and the institutional augmentation that occurs to allow for the coexistence of news nerds. This work follows the call of management scholars Trish Reay and C. R. Hinings to examine institutional change during moments of restructuring, as opposed to focusing on explanations of the sources of the disruption.[1] As such, data were collected to capture the critical period of change from 2011 to 2020, during which the profession of journalism and the news industry at large were in the midst of grappling with destabilization—most pertinent to this discussion, emerging roles and skill sets resulting from ongoing technological jolts and associated disruption of news production and consumption processes.

My goal was to tell a story that blends individual, organizational, and institutional accounts to explain how and why the profession of journalism is undergoing institutional augmentation—an institutional change process that has allowed for the emergence, establishment, and coexistence of news nerds as a qualitatively and quantitatively distinct and supplementary professional journalism institution. As journalism scholars Alfred Hermida and Mary Lynn Young note in their 2019 book on data journalism, an assessment of the profession at this point provides insight into journalism decades after the impact of digital journalism and some of the first disruptive technologies.[2]

In order to accomplish this goal, I use a mixed-method approach, which enables the combination of qualitative and quantitative methods and highlights the collective strengths of each while compensating for individual weaknesses of each individual approach.[3] Furthermore, the use of a variety of data sources with the mixed methods enables a triangulation process[4] of comparison, analysis, and interpretation that provides a more nuanced understanding of the institutional

Table A.1. **Mixed methods research design.**

Method	Data Source	Analytical Procedure
Qualitative data analysis	- Interviews - Archival materials (e.g., industry press articles and reports) - Professional conference programs - Industry awards - Participant observation	- Narrative coding
Social network analysis	- Case study of NYC news organization employee work histories	- Longitudinal network visualizations and measures (e.g., degree centrality and betweenness centrality)
Quantitative data analysis	- Journalist employment histories - News organization degree centrality scores - Public organizational data - Industry awards	- Binomial logistic regression - Multivariate linear regression - Content analysis

augmentation of news nerds research phenomena. Table A.1 presents a summary of the mixed methods, data sources, and analytical procedures, which are then discussed in the following subsections in greater detail.

Data Sources

The main data sources for the book include the following: news industry trade press articles, semi-structured interviews with professional journalists, publicly available employment histories, journalist job listings, professional journalism conference programs, news industry award archives, participant observation of industry conferences, and two organizational research databases. Data collection procedures for each of these sources are outlined in the following sections.

Industry Publications

Building upon earlier work examining trade press coverage of the journalism and news industry, I built the industry materials data set from the archives of leading news industry trade publications, including Columbia Journalism Review

Table A.2. **List of industry materials publications.**

Publication Source	Number of Articles
Columbia Journalism Review	57
Digiday	66
Nieman Journalism Lab	108
Poynter Online	81
Various industry documents	10
Total	322

(CJR), Digiday, Nieman Journalism Lab, and Poynter Online. To explore trends in news nerds and the profession of journalism, I focused on key terms representative of the changing nature of a professional journalist. The selection of terms was further guided by discussions with interview subjects. The list included articles that referenced one of more of the following keywords: "data," "application," "analytics," "programmer," "platform," "engagement," "interactive," "graphics," "social," "mobile," or "visual" co-occurring with "journalist," "journalism," "editor," or "team." A full list of publication sources and article counts is provided in Table A.2.

Interviews

Semi-structured, in-depth interviews were conducted with professional news nerds. Interviews are often used in studies of institutional change and professions to provide detailed illustrations and further understanding of change processes.[5] In general, the goal of the interviews is to get a broad sense of the news industry's approach and response to recent transformation, especially with regard to change in the profession of journalism. Furthermore, interviews focused on the development of news nerds and the qualities that signify both news nerds and leading news nerd organizations. Snowball sampling was used to recruit additional interviewees; each interviewee was asked to nominate additional subjects.

In total, 25 interviews with professional journalists were conducted over a period of four years. The objective in selecting interview subjects was to recruit participants from a wide array of news organizations. Interview subjects represented a range of news sectors including print, broadcast, and digital-native news organizations. Legacy organizations such as *The Wall Street Journal*, as well as newer entrant organizations such as Vox were both included. Interview subjects also represented a range of organizational sizes from regional news organizations such as the *Tampa Bay Times* to larger news organizations with international operations such as Bloomberg.

Journalist titles varied substantially across interview subjects and included references, for example, to apps, data, development, engagement, interactive, and visual journalism. The majority of interview subjects were at the level of editor or manager. Approximately half of the interview subjects came from a traditional educational background in journalism; other educational backgrounds ranged from art and design to computer science and physics. Table A.3 provides a list of interview subjects along with corresponding organizations and positions, as well as interview date.

Table A.3. **List of interview subjects.**

Name	Position	Organization	Date
Anonymous A	Mobile Editor	Digital-native news organization	October 7, 2016
Anonymous B	News Editor	Digital-native news organization	October 7, 2016
Anonymous C	Visual Journalist	Print news organization	April 24, 2017
Sarah Slobin	Things Editor	Quartz	May 22, 2017
Meredith Broussard	Assistant Professor, Arthur L. Carter Journalism Institute	New York University	May 23, 2017
Erin Medley	Director, Editorial and Audience Development	TVGM Holdings	June 1, 2017
Rachel Schallom	Project Manager	*Wall Street Journal*	June 1, 2017
Anonymous D	Journalist	Independent	June 2, 2017
Brian Boyer	Head of Product of Operations	Spirited Media	June 5, 2017
Elaine Piniat	Audience Engagement Editor	Newsday Media Group	June 9, 2017
David Eads	News Applications Developer	ProPublica	June 13, 2017
Courtney (CJ) Sinner	Data Graphics Producer	*Star Tribune*	June 13, 2017
Julia Wolfe	Visual Journalist	FiveThirtyEight	June 16, 2017
Madi Alexander	Data Journalism Reporter	Bloomberg BNA	June 29, 2017

Table A.3. **Continued**

Name	Position	Organization	Date
Adam Playford	Investigations Editor	*Tampa Bay Times*	July 2, 2017
Sisi Wei	Deputy Editor of News Applications	ProPublica	July 6, 2017
Alvin Chang	Senior Graphics Reporter	Vox	July 10, 2017
Anonymous E	Interactive News Engineer	Print news organization	July 12, 2017
Anonymous F	Design Editor	Print news organization	July 14, 2017
Anonymous G	VP of Product	Broadcast news organization	July 17, 2017
Tyler Fisher	Deputy Director, Technology	News Catalyst	July 22, 2019
Jeremy Bowers	Director of Engineering	*Washington Post*	July 19, 2019
Brittany Mayes	Graphics Reporter	*Washington Post*	August 1, 2019
Ben Welsh	Editor, Data and Graphics	*Los Angeles Times*	September 9, 2020
Anonymous H	Data Editor	Nonprofit news organization	September 10, 2020

All interviews were recorded, transcribed, and aggregated into a database for coding and analysis. Initial interviewees were strategically identified based on a wide network of professional contacts. Subsequent subjects were identified based on recommendations from the initial interviews, which enabled a snowball sampling process.

On average, interviews lasted 30 minutes. Interview subjects were initially contacted via email. Interviews were conducted and recorded mostly via VOIP or mobile phone. Subjects were not offered compensation. They were offered the option of anonymity. Identifying information is provided if a participant waived the right to anonymity.

Journalism Conference Programs

Building upon earlier work that examined professional organizations and conferences as an indicator of industry change, I constructed the journalism conference programs database from the archives of three leading annual professional

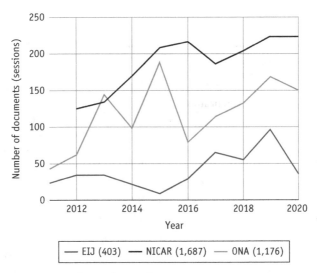

Figure A.1 Session counts by conference by year.

journalism conferences held by the National Institute for Computer-Assisted Reporting (NICAR), the Online News Association (ONA), and the Society for Professional Journalists (SPJ). To explore changes in the ways that the profession itself grapples with and evaluates the utility of news nerds, I collected conference program session titles and descriptions from each of the three conferences every year from 2011 to 2020, which led to a corpus of 3,266 documents (i.e., session descriptions).

Data include the full text from every conference program from between 2011 and 2020 in each of the three main annual U.S. professional journalism conferences (NICAR, EIJ, ONA). This yields a corpus of 3,268 conference program sessions including 14,819 distinct terms and more than 140,730 words exclusive of "stop words" such as articles and conjunctions. Stop words were removed with tidytext packages[6] including dplyr in the open-source R framework.[7]

Figure A.1 depicts the number of documents (i.e., sessions) in each conference program in each year. The analysis focuses on the key topics of "data," "analytics," and "product." Both the title and text of all conference sessions were analyzed for term prevalence.

News Industry Award Winners

Building upon earlier work examining news industry award winners as a window into the state of exemplary journalism, I constructed the news industry award winners database from the archives of two leading annual journalism award competitions: the Pulitzer Prize and the Online Journalism Awards. To explore trends in exemplary professional journalists and journalism, I collected data from the Explanatory Reporting and Feature Writing categories in both the Pulitzer Prize awards and the Online Journalism Awards from 2010 through 2020. For the Online Journalism Awards, each category was further broken down into large, medium, and small newsroom subcategories, which led to a database of 59 award citations.

Participant Observation

Over the past several years, I attended a number of industry events that focused on the topic of change in the profession of journalism and transformation in the news industry at large. These events included, for example, the Journalism and Silicon Valley conference (November 2015), the World Media Economics and Management conference (May 2016), the Future of Augmented Journalism (May 2017), SRCCON (July 2019), and ONA (August 2020). This combination of workshops and conferences provided useful arenas to conduct participant observation of professional journalists and industry change and helped add context to this research.

Employment Histories

A sample set of news organizations was created as a representative case study of professional journalist employment histories. Analysis was restricted to news organizations headquartered in New York City. The NYC context provides a test bed for examining ongoing change related to professional journalists due to the diversity of organizations in NYC, the size of the media market, and the interaction of news organizations with other collocated industries.[8]

The sample set of news organizations was generated using CisionPoint, which is a global commercial media database with over 1.6 million records considered to be representative of the journalist population[9] and previously utilized in research examining professional journalists.[10] CisionPoint allows for the search and filtering of news organizations by a variety of input variables. A search for U.S. newspapers, television networks, and websites headquartered in the NYC area that covered news and published on a daily and/or continuous basis resulted in a sample list of 15 organizations that also have a company profile page on professional networking site LinkedIn. Published lists are often used as a viable sampling frame when it is not possible to get an accurate count of the total population.[11]

The 15 focal organizations are ABC News, Buzzfeed, CBS News, Daily Beast, Fox News, the Huffington Post, Mic, MSNBC, NBC News, *New York Daily News*, *The New York Times*, NowThis, Patch, Slate, and *The Wall Street Journal*. These companies all perform important news functions, but they are not all traditional, legacy newspaper companies. Some of the organizations included in this sample are primarily print news organizations, others produce broadcast news, and some are digital-native news organizations. In aggregate, this sample represents a cross section of news sectors and organizations providing news in the NYC area.

Five are broadcast news organizations, three are print news organizations, and seven are digital-native news organizations, which together provide a sample that covers the three main sectors of the news industry. Ten of the companies are public or owned by a public company, while the remaining organizations operate under some form of private structure. The founding dates vary from 1851 (*The New York Times*) to 2012 (NowThis); six of the organizations were founded after 2000.

Additional summary data on this sample of NYC news organizations and the professional journalists are provided in Table A.4. The male to female ratio ranged from 0.54 at the Huffington Post to 1.31 at Slate ($M = 0.87, SD = 0.24$). The percentage of employees with an undergraduate degree in journalism ranged from 4% at NowThis to 31% at Fox News ($M = 20.31, SD = 0.07$). The percentage of employees with a graduate degree in journalism ranged from 4% at Patch to 19% at *The Wall Street Journal* ($M = 10.78, SD = 0.04$).

Information on professional journalists and employment histories of individuals working for the sample news organizations were created by aggregating public data sources such as Pew Research Center's State of the News Media, the American Society for News Editors Newsroom Employment Census, and LinkedIn, a professional networking site with 500 million global users[12] that contains information about a substantial portion of the U.S. workforce.[13] Employment histories on LinkedIn contain information about labor markets and professional workforces such as prior employers, job roles, skills, and education.[14]

Prior research has utilized LinkedIn data to examine the technological professionalization of political campaign workforces such as in scholar Daniel Kreiss's book *Prototype Politics*[15] as well as to analyze the robustness of the information on workforce mobility as compared to patent information.[16] In fact, management scholars Chunmian Ge, Ke-Wei Huang, and Ivan Png found that LinkedIn was a more reliable source of career histories than patent tracking, with a 90% accuracy rate as compared to 70%.[17]

A search was conducted for each of the organizations in the data set and employee histories were recorded manually in a separate database. Data

Table A.4. Summary of employment data for sample news organizations.

	Sector	Founding Date	Corporate Structure	Employees	M:F Ratio	Undergrad J-Degree	Graduate J-Degree
ABC News	Broadcast	1948	Public (Disney)	463	0.87	21.81%	7.99%
Buzzfeed	Digital	2006	Private	194	0.58	21.65%	9.79%
CBS News	Broadcast	1927	Public	359	0.91	18.11%	11.98%
Daily Beast	Digital	2008	Public (IAC)	42	0.91	11.90%	14.29%
Fox News	Broadcast	1996	Public (Fox)	331	0.66	30.82%	5.74%
Huffington Post	Digital	2005	Public (Verizon)	618	0.54	11.00%	7.93%
Mic	Digital	2011	Private	92	0.67	23.91%	6.52%
MSNBC	Broadcast	1996	Public	211	0.63	20.38%	9.95%
NBC News	Broadcast	1939	Public (Comcast)	310	0.68	25.16%	13.23%
New York Daily News	Print	1919	Private	115	1.25	28.70%	12.17%
New York Times	Print	1851	Public	393	0.90	22.39%	15.78%
NowThis	Digital	2012	Private	24	1.09	4.17%	16.67%
Patch	Digital	2007	Private	45	1.14	20.00%	4.44%
Slate	Digital	1996	Public (Graham Holdings)	30	1.31	20.00%	6.67%
Wall Street Journal	Print	1889	Public (News Corp)	360	0.96	24.72%	18.61%
Average		48 (years)		239	0.87	20.31%	10.78%

collection for the employment histories began in February 2016 and concluded in July 2016. The overall data collection approach was validated by cross referencing the number of employees listed across data sources including the CisionPoint database, Pew Research reports, and Muck Rack. The data verification is provided in Table A.5.

Position job titles, organizations, and dates of employment were collected for the employment histories of each employee at the sample news organizations. Educational information, including undergraduate degree and graduate degree (when applicable), was also collected for each employee. Immediately following completion of collection and recording, data were de-identified and anonymized.

At this point, organizations and positions in the data set were categorically coded in order to summarize the data. Organizations were coded by industry and positions were coded by general function. Industry codes were assigned based on common mission as envisioned by a combination of the organization's LinkedIn company page and corporate website. Industry codes include broadcast media, consulting, education, entertainment, finance, government, health, marketing, newspapers, nonprofits, online media, publishing, research, retail, technology, and other.

Position codes were created through an iterative process of code generation, undertaken by the researcher and verified through interviews with journalists.

Table A.5. **Data verification for using LinkedIn.**

	LinkedIn	CisionPoint	2016 Pew Data	Muck Rack
ABC News	463	201	–	333
Buzzfeed	194	124	170	270
CBS News	359	247	–	269
Daily Beast	42	54	50	62
Fox News	331	233	1272	241
Huffington Post	618	159	575	199
Mic	92	44	13	51
MSNBC	211	102	600	159
NBC News	310	220	–	469
NY Daily News	115	102	–	104
NY Times	393	659	3588	868
NowThis	24	5	–	12
Patch	45	46	50	25
Slate	30	50	50	61
Wall Street Journal	360	484	–	908

Position codes include admin, analyst, audience, audio, blogger, broadcaster, camera, consultant, copy editor, copy writer, curator, data, design, developer, development, director, editor, engagement, founder, mobile design, mobile developer, mobile editor, mobile manager, mobile producer, online admin, online analyst, online broadcaster, online camera, online copy editor, online copy writer, online data, online design, online developer, online director, online editor, online engineer, online manager, online operations, online producer, online reporter, online research, online strategy, online writer, operations, platform, producer, product, programmer, reporter, research, social media, strategy, technology, writer, and other.

The position for each work history was coded to reflect the general function on two levels: first, to reflect general positions such as producer, reporter, writer, editor, and so on, and second, to further understanding of the development of news nerd jobs across the news industry. Thus, newsroom job titles were also assigned one of two codes: traditional or news nerd. The traditional category encompasses both traditional and online editorial, reporter, and support positions within the newsroom such as editor, journalist, producer, and writer. The news nerd category reflects those technological developments that came after the transition from print to online news, which became specifically evident through the interview process and include the rise of big data, audience engagement metrics, application programming and software development, and social and mobile platforms. news nerd positions include, for example, data journalist, engagement editor, and news applications developer. This general coding scheme was further verified through multiple interviews with professional journalists.

Job listings. To gain a better sense of change in journalist positions from 2011 through 2016, job advertisements were collected and analyzed. Job advertisements are textual representations of industry labor markets,[18] especially useful as indicators of change.[19] Job advertisements have been used in earlier research aimed at understanding changing job positions and skill sets in the news industry.[20] A leading database of journalism jobs was acquired; however, as part of the data-sharing agreement, identifying information from the job database has been kept confidential. The database provides seven years of data (2010–2016) and includes approximately 8,000 listings of journalism job openings. Each listing includes a time stamp, job title, employer, and job description. The listings were also further coded to reflect traditional versus news nerd positions according to the established coding scheme utilized on the employment histories and verified by professional journalists.

Organizational research databases. Additional data including company founding date and revenue of the 15 focal news organizations were collected from two databases: PrivCo and MarketLine. PrivCo is a database that tracks private organizations and thus was used for information on those organizations in the sample that are privately owned. MarketLine is a business information database for public companies and was thus used to collect information on those organizations in the sample that are publicly owned. The Rutgers University library provided access to both databases while I was a doctoral student.

Qualitative Data Analysis: Archival Research

A qualitative analysis was conducted in parallel on both the interview data and the archival industry press data in order to provide a contextualization of institutional change with regard to the journalism profession. Data from the participant observations of workshops and conferences were also used to confirm interpretation of events and further reliability.[21] In this way, data attend to both internal and external (organizational) material. In other words, interviews were conducted with professional journalists and articles were written by an external, public audience.

All interview transcripts, trade press articles, and industry reports were uploaded into NVivo, a qualitative software program.[22] NVivo facilitates the organization of texts for close-reading, detailed note taking, and coding and is thus utilized in qualitative analysis of text materials.[23] Together, these documents formed a data set that was read and coded iteratively according to both data and theory with the goal of identifying emergent themes and meaningful theoretical dimensions.[24] This analysis was used to contextualize the institutional change process related to professional journalists.

The analysis was conducted in two stages. First, a strategic narrative approach[25] was used to analyze change in professional journalists and the development of news nerds from 2011 through 2016. Data were first organized chronologically, generating a sequence of events and coherent narrative. Of particular interest was the development of news nerds as related to traditional journalists, as well as both internal and external response to this new form of professional journalists. An historical narrative was assembled once no new evidence emerged from the data.[26] The narrative summarized the key events and key players related to professional journalists and change. This approach enabled a reconstruction and contextualization of events related to the development of news nerds as a new form of professional journalists, as well as to the more general process of institutional change in the news industry.

Next, data were coded with the Greenwood et al. six-stage model[27] in mind, which allowed for a theoretical contextualization of strategies regarding institutional change in the journalist profession. For example, text from a 2012 article in the Columbia Journalism Review discussing the opportunities for innovation related to data expertise in the news industry tending to come from outside the field was tagged as "change from outside"[28] and categorized as an example of the deinstitutionalization stage. A quote from one news nerd discussing his experience as "a convert" being a software developer from the open data community was coded as "change from outside" and categorized as an example of change from outside the traditional boundaries of the professional field. As another illustration, a quote from one news nerd on the relevance of Pulitzer Prize award successes was coded as "cognitive legitimacy" and thus an example of the theorization stage of institutional change. Further, text from a 2016 Nieman Journalism Lab article on the revenue, grant, and award successes of ProPublica's news applications team[29] was also tagged as "legitimization" and thus an example of the theorization stage of institutional change.

Social Network Analysis: Network Histories

A case study of public employment histories (as explicated above) was collected to create an employment network of NYC area journalists from 2011 through 2015.[30] An employment network lends itself to social network analysis (SNA), which is widely used in studying organizational change[31] to examine the composition of a workforce over time, and the movement of professionals between different positions, organizations, and industries.

More specifically, SNA is a research method and theoretical approach that enables the examination of the connection between two entities based on a common relationship.[32] In order to analyze the employment history data as network data, it was necessary to convert the information from a database format to a network format. Each line of data in the employment database contains a unique identification number, job position, company, tenure, position code, and company industry code.

First, data were transformed into a two-mode affiliation network of the aggregated data from 2011 through 2015; later, subnetworks were created for each year. In network terminology, nodes are the vertices, and ties are the connections between those vertices. The two-mode network contains two types of vertices (e.g., journalists and organizations). In this case, a "1" was used to indicate that a journalist worked at a particular organization and a "0" was used to indicate that no relationship existed.

Next, a one-mode network of organizations-by-organizations (i.e., one type of vertex) was created from the original two-mode affiliation network of journalists-by-organizations (i.e., two types of vertices). Network packages including statnet[33] and igraph[34] were used in the open-source R framework[35] to conduct matrix multiplication and transform the two-mode network into the one-mode network of organizations. For example, in this one-mode network if Employee A works for *The New York Times*, and then in 2014 leaves *The New York Times* to go work for the Huffington Post, it would be possible to say that there is a relationship between *The New York Times* and the Huffington Post based on the movement of an employee from one company to the other.

While those networks provide insight into the evolution of the journalist profession as a whole, the second goal of this analytical task is to better understand news nerds as compared to traditional journalists. Thus, two subnetworks were generated: first, a network of only jobs coded as news nerd, and second, a network of only jobs coded as traditional. These networks were utilized to examine the organizational leaders and industry origins of news nerds as compared to traditional journalists.

While insight into the organizational leaders is gleaned from two-mode affiliation networks of journalists-by-organizations, insight into industry origins requires further network transformation. Here, one-mode networks were created to visualize the relationship between the current industry of each news nerd job in the data set and the industry of the prior job for each current news nerd. For example, if Employee A is currently in a news nerd position in digital-native news, and had a previous position in technology, it would be possible to say that there is a relationship between digital-native news and technology based on the movement of a news nerd from one industry to the other. This industry network was examined for news nerd to news nerd transitions and then compared to traditional to news nerd transitions.

A variety of network measures and visualizations were generated using the igraph package in the open-source R framework and in Gephi, an open-source network exploration and visualization tool was used for network visualization.[36] Together with descriptive statistics, these measures were used to examine the employment network of professional journalists over time from 2011 through 2015.

Quantitative Data Analysis: News Nerds and News Nerd Organizations

As discussed in Chapter 4, two regressions were conducted to better understand news nerds and news nerd organizations. First, I conducted a multiple linear regression to better understand legitimacy of news nerds at the organizational level. Next, I conducted a binomial logistic regression to better understand the role of legitimacy of news nerds at the actor (i.e., professional) level.

Multiple Linear Regression

In order to conduct the multiple linear regression, all data were collected and tracked in an Excel spreadsheet, which was then imported into the Statistical Package for Social Sciences (SPSS) Version 22 for analysis. Data were collected for the following variables:

Dependent variable—Degree centrality within the news nerd network. Degree centralities for each of the 15 sample news organizations within the news nerd network were measured and recorded. These measures were calculated for the aggregated networks over time and were normalized to allow for comparison.

Pragmatic legitimacy. Pragmatic legitimacy was measured as the number of news nerd positions under each organization in the job listings data set. Recall that pragmatic legitimacy involves the linking of something new with economic outcomes. In the case of the profession of journalism, pragmatic legitimacy of news nerds can be signaled, for example, through the dedication of resources to news nerd job positions. For each organization, the number of news nerd positions was then divided by the total number of positions in the data set in an effort to normalize the measure.

Age. Founding dates for each organization were collected using information from the PrivCo database (for private organizations) and the MarketLine database (for public organizations). A variable was created for organizational age that measures years in operation by subtracting the founding date from 2017.

Size. Organizational size was measured by the number of journalists for each organization as listed in the CisionPoint database.

Cognitive legitimacy. Cognitive legitimacy was measured as the number of articles for each organization in the trade press data set. Press coverage is an indicator for organizational legitimacy[37] as it increases public knowledge and awareness.[38] This is true specifically in the case of the news industry in which authority, power, and control are derived from external perceptions of legitimacy.[39] In addition, a search was conducted for the total number of articles mentioning each organization in all four of the main publication sources (CJR, Digiday, Nieman Lab, and Poynter). For each organization, the number of articles in the trade press data set was then divided by the total number of articles in the main publication sources to garner comparable measures of news nerd related legitimacy.

Control variables—Revenue. Utilizing information from PrivCo (for private organizations) and MarketLine (for public organizations), 2016 revenues for each organization were collected and recorded.

Table A.6. **Correlation table including means and standard deviations.**

	Mean	SD	1	2	3	4	5
1. Revenue	2,333.44	3,342.04	—	−0.26	−0.24	.520*	0.31
2. Cognitive legitimacy	0.03	0.03	—	—	−0.23	−0.36	−0.24
3. Pragmatic legitimacy	0.08	0.16	—	—	—	0.21	0.33
4. Age	49.47	51.82	—	—	—	—	0.45
5. Size	182.00	178.63	—	—	—	—	—

$N = 15;$ * $= p < 0.05$

Correlations were examined prior to running the regression. They are presented along with the means and standard deviations of each variable in Table A.6. Goodness of fit measures (ANOVA) were also used to validate the results of the regression.

Binomial Logistic Regression

In order to conduct the binomial logistic regression, all data were collected and tracked in an Excel spreadsheet, which was then imported into the SPSS Version 22 for analysis. Data were collected for the following variables:

Dependent variable I—news nerd. The dependent variable for the first binomial logistic regression is a dichotomous code reflecting news nerd employment. Journalists were coded as "1" if the current position was a news nerd job and "0" if it was non-news nerd. There are 150 current news nerds in the data set.

Dependent variable II—Traditional journalist. The dependent variable for the second binomial logistic regression is a dichotomous code reflecting traditional journalist employment. Journalists were coded as "1" if the current position was traditional and "0" if it was non-traditional. There are 3,437 current traditional journalists in the data set.

Education. The major (undergraduate degree) of each journalist was recorded and coded to reflect one of 11 categories guided by the National Center for Education Statistics: journalism (including news and media); communication (including advertising and public relations); business (e.g., accounting, finance, management, and economics) information and computer science; other social sciences (e.g., anthropology, sociology, psychology); other humanities (e.g., art history, literature, English); natural sciences (e.g., biology, chemistry, physics); visual and performing arts (e.g., fashion, theater, film); engineering; math and statistics; and other.

In order to test the education variable in a binomial logistic regression, it was transformed into 11 separate dummy variables within the SPSS program.[40]

Graduate education. Graduate education was utilized as a dichotomous variable. Journalists without a graduate degree were coded as "0." Journalists with a graduate degree were coded as "1."

Graduate education in journalism. Graduate education, specifically in a journalism program was also utilized as a dichotomous variable. Journalists without a graduate degree in journalism were coded as "0." Journalists with a graduate degree in journalism were coded as "1."

Years in industry. The number of years since undergraduate graduation was subtracted from the current year (2017). If no graduation year was listed, the start year of the first recorded job was used in the calculation. Years in industry ranged from 1 to 65 ($M = 10.18$, $SD = 8.90$).

Prior industry. The industry of the job prior to the current journalist job was recorded based on the industry coding of the employment history data set outlined in Chapter 3. Six prior industries were present in the data set, including broadcast news, digital news, print news, entertainment, publishing, and technology. In order to test the prior industry variable in a binomial logistic regression, it was transformed into six separate dummy variables within the SPSS program.

Industry diversity. The number of unique industries in the employment history for each journalist was recorded. Industry diversity ranged from 1 to 6 ($M = 1.05$, $SD = 0.76$).

News nerd jobs to total jobs. Lastly, this variable measures the ratio of news nerd jobs to total jobs for each journalist. As a ratio, the range was 0 to 1 ($M = 0.36$, $SD = 0.15$).

Assumptions regarding multicollinearity were tested and met prior to running the regressions. Correlations were examined for all variables and are presented in Table A.7. In addition, all variables had tolerance scores above 0.10 and variance inflation factor (VIF) scores between 1.00 and 2.50, thus meeting the assumptions for a logistic regression.[41] In addition, goodness of fit measures (e.g., Nagelkerke's pseudo R^2) were used to validate the results of the regression.

Analytical Limitations

While these analyses make important contributions to both existing theories of institutional change and existing knowledge about the profession of journalism, there are of course a number of limitations to the studies. While the archival

Table A.7. **Correlation matrix for independent variables.**

	1	2	3	4	5	6	7	8	9	10	11	12	13	14	15	16	17	18	19	20	21
1. GE	—																				
2. GE—J	0.66*	—																			
3. Years	-0.01	-0.02	—																		
4. Diversity	0.09*	0.07*	-0.01	—																	
5. NN/Tot.	0.03	0.03	-0.03	0.07*	—																
6. PI—B	-0.09*	-0.03	0.02	-0.18*	-0.08*	—															
7. PI—D	0.04*	0.04*	-0.01	0.14*	0.02	-0.26*	—														
8. PI—Print	0.06*	0.07*	0.01	0.01	0.05*	-0.31*	-0.14*	—													
9. PI—T	0.04*	0.01	0.01	0.23*	0.05*	-0.13*	-0.05*	-0.07*	—												
10. PI—E	0.02	0.01	0.02	0.21*	-0.01	-0.15*	-0.06*	-0.08*	-0.03	—											
11. PI—Pub	0.03	0.01	0.00	0.3*	-0.02	-0.21*	-0.09*	-0.11*	-0.04*	-0.05*	—										
12. Ed.—J	-0.09*	0.01	0.00	0.00	-0.02	0.15*	-0.02	0.01	-0.05*	-0.02	-0.04	—									
13. Ed.—C	-0.04*	-0.01	-0.01	-0.05*	-0.01	0.07*	-0.02	-0.07*	0.00	0.00	-0.04*	-0.22*	—								
14. Ed.—B	0.02	0.00	0.01	-0.04*	0.08*	-0.01	-0.03	-0.02	0.00	-0.02	-0.03	-0.15*	-0.07*	—							
15. Ed.—CS	0.03	-0.01	-0.02	-0.01	0.05*	-0.04	-0.01	0.02	0.01	-0.02	0.01	-0.05*	-0.03	-0.02	—						
16. Ed.—SS	0.09*	0.03	-0.02	0.02	0.02	-0.05*	0.04	-0.03	0.02	-0.01	0.02	-0.23*	-0.12*	-0.08*	-0.03	—					
17. Ed.—H	0.15*	0.09*	0.00	0.07*	-0.01	-0.14*	0.07*	0.09*	0.05*	0.01	0.07*	-0.34*	-0.17*	-0.11*	-0.04*	-0.18*	—				
18. Ed.—NS	0.07*	0.02	-0.02	-0.02	0.01	-0.05*	0.03	-0.05*	0.02	-0.01	0.02	-0.08*	-0.04*	-0.03	-0.01	-0.04*	-0.07*	—			
19. Ed.—A	-0.01	-0.05*	0.01	0.06*	-0.02	-0.02	-0.02	-0.04*	0.02	0.07*	-0.01	-0.19*	-0.01*	-0.06*	-0.02	-0.01*	-0.15*	-0.04	—		
20. Ed.—E	0.05*	-0.01	0.01	-0.03	0.04*	-0.01	-0.01	0.03	-0.01	-0.01	-0.01	-0.03	-0.01	-0.01	0.00	-0.01	-0.02	-0.01	-0.01	—	
21. Ed.—M	0.00	-0.02	0.02	0.01	0.06*	-0.01	-0.02	0.02	-0.01	-0.01	0.01	-0.03	-0.02	-0.01	0.00	-0.02	-0.02	-0.01	-0.01	0.00	—

Note: Pearson's correlation coefficient, r; $N = 3,587$; $*p < .01$

industry materials and interviews were analyzed as representations of the news industry, the employment history data and network histories do not capture the full scale of the news industry.

The data set, which represents professional journalists at a sample of 15 NYC news organizations, was compared with the 2016 American Society of News Editors (ASNE) survey of newsrooms. On a whole, the sample of professional journalists used in this study was somewhat skewed toward female journalists. ASNE (2016) survey results found that 61% of full-time journalists were men and 39% were women. The data used in this study has 46% men and 54% women. Indeed, the NYC news market is a likely media bubble, and while it may not be completely representative of newsrooms across the country, it serves as a fairly large representation of professional journalists.[42] A more comprehensive sample would capture a wider range of professional journalist employment histories and thus more accurately reflect the industry as a whole. As such, this is a potential and important avenue for future research.

Furthermore, although these 15 NYC news organizations resulted in a large sample of professional journalists ($N = 3,587$) for the regression testing news nerds, the regression that tests news nerd organizations was thus limited to a sample of 15. This is clearly a very small sample size; a more comprehensive sample would further establish greater generalizability of the findings reported here in exploring the process of institutional change and, specifically, the factors that contribute to the probability of a news organization being a leader in news nerds. Future research should explore this by expanding on the case study.

The regression examining institutional change at the actor level and testing the factors that contribute to the likelihood of a journalist being a news nerd also has an additional limitation. The odds ratio for the news nerd jobs to total jobs variable is large, which suggests a high correlation with the dependent variable ($r = 0.83$, $p < 0.01$) and the possibility that the outcome (news nerd) is a virtual certainty. In essence, the large odds ratio implies that there is a notably low probability that one would currently be a news nerd without ever having a previous news nerd job. The overall model, however, is not significant without some representation of the number of news nerd jobs in a journalist's work history. Furthermore, this variable met the collinearity thresholds, which implies that it is suitable. Indeed, the news nerd ratio variable was dominant in the analysis and therefore more variables should be included; however, the available data were limited for this present study and as such, this model is a first attempt at understanding the factors that contribute to the likelihood that a journalist is a news nerd and requires further fine-tuning.

In addition, the case study findings are in part based on the collection and analysis of data from an online professional social networking site. Profiles on these social sites are not agreed upon historical record; rather, they are a self-reported presentation of one's work and education history. Profiles are voluntary and possibly distorted;[43] furthermore, data can be easily deleted or changed. In addition, there are different incentives for users to participate on the website, which leads to concerns regarding an unknown sampling frame.[44] Such limitations can potentially lead to estimation bias; however, prior research suggests such concerns can be mitigated with large sample sizes and correlations with other data sources as is the case here.

The case study data set also has an inherent limitation with regards to longitudinal analysis. The data are less complete with each prior year. This is simply a factor of the way that LinkedIn functions. For example, we have generally complete data on current BuzzFeed employees; however, with each prior year, the picture is less complete. As such, historical references can be used to estimate sample completion. In the case of BuzzFeed during the first year of change (2011), the data set is about 20% complete. Thus, this method of data collection is limited as far as a snapshot of 2011, but it is also the best picture available of the employment trajectory of news nerds and the journalist profession more broadly.

Finally, the assessment of news nerds as compared to traditional journalists is grounded in the coding of job titles. While job titles are an important and recognized representation of the responsibilities, knowledge, skills, and abilities an employee is likely to possess, they do not always reflect an employee's "unique value."[45] These concerns were mitigated with multiple rounds of iterative coding verified through interviews with professional journalists.

Indeed, the data are not perfect. However, the mixed-method approach and the combination of a wide variety of data sources reflecting multiple levels of perspective offers a robust view from which to analyze institutional change. The triangulation of findings further supports a confidant assessment of institutional change resulting in institutional augmentation in the profession of journalism for news nerds.

Notes

Introduction

 1. Welsh, 2020, personal communication.
 2. Sinner, 2017, personal communication.
 3. Chang, 2017, personal communication.
 4. Williams & Martin, 1911.
 5. Hansen, 1976.
 6. Wickenden, 1991.
 7. Lewis & Usher, 2013.
 8. Hagel III & Brown, 2017.
 9. Bell, 2016.
10. Barthel et al., 2020.
11. Barthel et al., 2020.
12. Barthel et al., 2020.
13. Barthel, 2018.
14. Grieco, 2020.
15. Ivancsics & Hansen, 2019.
16. Ryley, 2021.
17. Ryley, 2021.
18. Cherubini, 2017.
19. Meyer & Rowan, 1977.
20. Scott, 1995.
21. Reay et al., 2017.

Chapter 1

 1. Welsh, 2020, personal communication.
 2. Singer, 2003; Usher, 2016.
 3. Reay et al., 2017, p. 1044; Scott, 2001.
 4. Singer, 2003.
 5. Deuze, 2005.
 6. Powers, 2012.
 7. Ornebring & Mellado, 2016.
 8. Carlson, 2017.
 9. See, e.g. Deuze, 2005; Ferrucci & Vos, 2017.
10. Lewis & Westlund, 2015b.

11. Zelizer, 1995.
12. Lowrey, 2002.
13. Lewis & Westlund, 2016.
14. Anderson et al., 2014, p. 34.
15. Anderson et al., 2014; Tushman & Anderson, 1986.
16. Usher, 2016, p. 18.
17. Parasie & Dagiral, 2012; Tourino, 2017.
18. Ananny & Crawford, 2015.
19. Zamith, 2019.
20. Howard, 2014 p. 4.
21. Hermida & Young, 2019.
22. Anderson, 2011.
23. Belair-Gagnon & Holton, 2018.
24. Neheli, 2018, p. 1041.
25. Creech & Mendelson, 2015.
26. Bell et al., 2017, p. 16.
27. Lewis & Westlund, 2016, p. 347.
28. On Tampa Bay Times' "Failure Factories" see http://www.tampabay.com/projects/2015/investigations/pinellas-failure-factories/
29. https://www.facebook.com/wsj/posts/10153654004448128
30. http://www.nytimes.com/projects/2012/snow-fall/
31. https://www.nytimes.com/interactive/2020/world/coronavirus-maps.html
32. https://www.propublica.org/newsapps
33. Li, 2013.
34. See, e.g., the book *Apostles of Certainty,* in which Anderson (2018) provides a compelling account of the rise of data and computational methods in journalism over the last two centuries and touches upon the historical and material perspectives this phenomenon has moving forward.
35. Hickson et al., 1971.
36. Pfeffer & Salancik, 1978.
37. Meyer & Rowan, 1977.
38. Scott, 1995, p. 33.
39. Meyer & Rowan, 1977.
40. Powell & DiMaggio, 1991.
41. Slack & Hinings, 1994.
42. Dacin et al., 2002.
43. Leblebici et al., 1991.
44. Marquis & Lounsbury, 2007.
45. Wright et al., 2017.
46. Cook, 2005; Schudson, 2002.
47. Lowrey, 2011.
48. Boczkowski, 2004.
49. Naldi & Picard, 2012.
50. Boczkowski, 2004.
51. Ryfe, 2012.
52. Ananny & Crawford, 2015; Lewis & Westlund, 2015a.
53. Kreiss & Saffer, 2017, p. 19.
54. Dickinson, 2007; Ornebring, 2009.
55. Leicht & Fennell, 2008.
56. Allison, 1986.
57. Abbott, 1988
58. Reay et al., 2017.
59. Muzio et al., 2013.

60. Glynn, 2008.
61. Leicht & Fennell, 2008.
62. Muzio et al., 2013.
63. Adler & Kwon, 2013.
64. Greenwood et al., 2002.
65. Meyer et al., 1990.
66. Maguire et al., 2004.
67. Smets et al., 2012, p. 877.
68. Greenwood et al., 2002.
69. Hardy & Maguire, 2008.
70. Leblebici et al., 1991.
71. Hardy & Maguire, 2008.
72. Tolbert & Zucker, 1996.
73. Greenwood et al. (2002) nest legitimization in a stage of theorization during which accounts of change are simplified in an effort to further adoption of new structures.
74. Suchman, 1995.
75. Bitektine, 2011, p. 152.
76. Suchman, 1995.
77. Greenwood et al., 2002, p. 60.
78. DiMaggio & Powell, 1991.
79. Suchman, 1995.
80. Greenwood et al., 2002.
81. Suchman, 1995.
82. Colyvas & Powell, 2006.
83. According to the Greenwood et al. (2002) model, pragmatic legitimacy is a consequence of diffusion, which signals an increase in shared understanding and planning that engenders routine. In the case of news nerds and the profession of journalism, however, pragmatic legitimacy occurs prior to full diffusion and institutionalization.
84. Lowrey, 2012.
85. Tolbert & Zucker, 1996.
86. Lee & Pennings, 2002.
87. DiMaggio & Powell, 1983.
88. Greenwood et al., 2002, p. 61.
89. Anonymous, personal communication, July 14, 2017.
90. Anonymous, personal communication, July 12, 201.
91. Bell et al., 2017, p. 16.
92. Young & Carson, 2018.
93. Usher, 2016, p. 3.
94. Kieser, 1994.
95. Betrand & Hughes, 2005; Astroff, 1988; Kosterich & Napoli, 2016.
96. Data collection for the employment histories began in February 2016 and concluded in July 2016 while I was a PhD student at Rutgers University. My PhD advisor, Matthew Weber, and I received generous grant funding through the Tow Center for Digital Journalism at Columbia University to create the data set. Four undergraduate research assistants at Rutgers also helped with data collection, including Priya Ashish, Akshar Patel, Samantha Nitting, and Abhisek Vyas.
97. See also, Kosterich & Weber (2019b) and (Kosterich et al., forthcoming).
98. Monge et al., 2008.
99. This is a substantive sample of journalists in the United States at the time of data collection. According to the American Society of News Editors (ASNE), there were 32,900 full-time journalists in 2015 (Doctor, 2015); this sample thus captures approximately 11% of U.S. journalists based on the ASNE estimate.

100. The size of each organization in the visualization corresponds to its degree centrality. A high degree of centrality generally indicates organizations that are likely to be more important within a network.

Chapter 2

1. Welsh, 2019, personal communication.
2. Greenwood et al., 2002.
3. Barthel, 2017.
4. Grueskin et al., 2011.
5. Grueskin et al., 2011.
6. Uberti, 2014.
7. Tourino, 2017.
8. Howard, 2014.
9. Howard, 2014.
10. Meyer, 1973.
11. Bell, 2012, p. 1.
12. Bell, 2015b.
13. Howard, 2014, p. ii.
14. Bell et al., 2017.
15. Rashidian et al., 2019.
16. Peters, 2012.
17. Foster, 2012, p. 6.
18. Bell, 2015a.
19. Bell et al., 2017.
20. Historical daily market capitalization values were generated with Capital IQ. Average values from May 18, 2012, through August 18, 2020, were calculated.
21. Bell et al., 2017.
22. Walker, 2019.
23. Newman et al., 2020.
24. Thomas, 2011, p. 1.
25. Carlson, 2017.
26. Newman et al., 2020.
27. Newman et al., 2020.
28. Moses, 2014.
29. Petre, 2015.
30. Bell et al., 2017.
31. Dixon, 2014.
32. Morrison, 2014.
33. Thompson, 2014.
34. Mitchell & Page, 2014.
35. Benes, 2016.
36. O'Donovan, 2014.
37. Wu, 2016.
38. Bunce, 2015.
39. Usher, 2013.
40. Hanusch, 2016.
41. Belair-Gagnon & Holton, 2018.
42. PrivCo, 2017.
43. Kosterich & Weber, 2019a.
44. Hasenpusch & Baumann, 2017.
45. Usher, 2017, Venture-backed News Startups and the Field of Journalism, *Digital Journalism*, 5(9): 1116–1133, DOI:10.1080/21670811.2016.1272064.

46. Medill School of Journalism, 2007.
47. Boyer, 2017, personal communication.
48. Boyer, 2017, personal communication.
49. Alexander, 2017, personal communication.
50. Boyer, 2017, personal communication.
51. Bowers, 2020, personal communication.
52. Gordon, 2018.
53. Bell, 2012.
54. Benton, 2012.
55. Welsh, 2020, personal communication.
56. opennews.org.
57. Benton, 2012, p. 2.
58. OpenNews, 2017.
59. Bell et al., 2017.
60. Bell, 2012.
61. Stray, 2012.
62. Sylvie, 2018; Young & Carson, 2018.
63. Hermida & Young, 2019.
64. Lowrey, 2002.
65. Zelizer, 1995.
66. Eldridge, 2019.
67. Eldridge, 2019, p. 858.
68. Holton & Belair-Gagnon, 2018, p. 72.
69. Zelizer, 1995.
70. Lowrey, 2002.
71. See, e.g., Deuze, 2003; Petre, 2015.
72. Tandoc, 2019.
73. Degree centrality is the number of connections that a node has with other nodes within the network. This measure is used to indicate a node's popularity or activity within the network (Wasserman & Faust, 1994) and can be used as a good proxy for the level of importance in a network (Cherven, 2015). In directed networks as opposed to undirected networks, it is possible to measure both in-degree the number of incoming ties and out-degree the number of outgoing ties centrality. Out-degree centrality measures were calculated with the degree routines in iGraph (see, Ognyanova, 2016).

Chapter 3

1. Medley, 2017, personal communication.
2. Anonymous news nerd, 2017, personal communication.
3. Anonymous news nerd, 2017, personal communication.
4. Waite, 2011, p. 1.
5. Wolfe, 2017, personal communication.
6. Anonymous news nerd, 2017, personal communication.
7. Greenwood et al., 2002.
8. Tolbert & Zucker, 1996, p. 181.
9. Dyer et al., 2011.
10. Boyles, 2016.
11. Fisher, 2019, personal communication.
12. Alikhan & Thompson, 2015, p. 2.
13. McDonald, 2019.
14. Wenzel, 2017.
15. Polgreen, 2014.
16. Weber, 2013.

17. Ingram, 2012.
18. McKenzie, 2013.
19. Myers, 2011.
20. Bell, 2012.
21. Oputu, 2014.
22. Bowers, 2020, personal communication.
23. Thomas, 2011.
24. Romenesko, 2012, p. 1.
25. Anonymous news nerd, 2017, personal communication.
26. Haughney, 2013, p. 2.
27. Usher, 2016.
28. Anonymous news nerd, 2017, personal communication.
29. Fisher, 2019, personal communication.
30. Welsh, 2020, personal communication.
31. Welsh, 2020, personal communication.
32. Welsh, 2020, personal communication.
33. Anonymous news nerd, 2016, personal communication.
34. Peters, 2012, p. 1.
35. Schallom, 2017, personal communication.
36. Anonymous, 2016, personal communication.
37. Playford, 2017, personal communication.
38. Wei, 2017, personal communication.
39. Sinner, 2017, personal communication.
40. Playford, 2017, personal communication.
41. Wei, 2017, personal communication.
42. Anonymous news nerd, 2017, personal communication.
43. Wei, 2017, personal communication.
44. Anonymous news nerd, 2017, personal communication.
45. Waite, 2011.
46. Fincham, 2012.
47. Symposium on Computation + Journalism, 2008.
48. Schallom, 2017, personal communication.
49. Howard, 2014.
50. Waite, 2011, p. 1.
51. Ellis, 2013, p. 3.

Chapter 4

1. Anonymous news nerd, 2016, personal communication.
2. Anonymous news nerd, 2016, personal communication.
3. Anonymous news nerd, 2016, personal communication.
4. Suchman, 1995.
5. Hallin & Mancini, 2004.
6. Splendore et al., 2016.
7. Benton, 2014.
8. Spinner, 2014.
9. Welsh, 2020, personal communication.
10. Chang, 2017, personal communication.
11. Anonymous news nerd, 2017, personal communication.
12. Berret & Phillips, 2016, p. 9.
13. Heravi, 2019.
14. Finberg, 2014.
15. Funt, 2014.

16. Lynch, 2015, pt 5, p. 36.
17. Hare, 2015.
18. Suchman, 1995.
19. Greenwood et al., 2002.
20. Bowers 2011, p. 1
21. Bilton, 2015.
22. Klein, 2016.
23. Welsh, 2020, personal communication.
24. Welsh, 2020, personal communication.
25. Wolfe, 2017 personal communication.
26. Alexander, 2017, personal communication.
27. Wolfe, 2017, personal communication.
28. Fisher, 2019, personal communication.
29. Welsh, 2020, Twitter thread, https://mobile.twitter.com/palewire/status/131672742685 7148416
30. Welsh, 2020, Twitter thread, https://mobile.twitter.com/palewire/status/131672742685 7148416
31. Welsh, 2020, Twitter thread, https://mobile.twitter.com/palewire/status/131672742685 7148416
32. Welsh, 2020, Twitter thread, https://mobile.twitter.com/palewire/status/131672742685 7148416
33. Alexander, 2017, personal communication.
34. Wolfe, 2017, personal communication.
35. Wei, 2017, personal communication.
36. Schallom, 2017, personal communication.
37. Hannan & Freeman, 1986.
38. Deephouse, 1996.
39. Anand & Watson, 2004.
40. Weber et al., 2016.
41. Pollack & Rindova, 2003.
42. Anand & Watson, 2004.
43. Schallom, 2017, personal communication.
44. OJA, 2015.
45. Redohl, 2017.
46. Klein, 2016, p. 2.
47. Anonymous, 2017, personal communication.
48. Hamilton, 2016, p. 44
49. Hamilton, 2004.
50. The baseline model for the test is as follows: $y_i = \beta_0 + \beta_1 X_{i1} + \beta_2 X_{i2} + \ldots + \beta_k X_{ip} + \varepsilon_i$ where y_i represents organizational leadership in news nerds, and there are k (in this case, 5) input variables, which are each associated with a regression coefficient β (Campbell, 2006).
51. Leech et al., 2011.
52. Bitektine, 2011; Kennedy, 2008; Weber et al., 2016.
53. Hannan & Freeman, 1986.
54. Hanitzsch & Vos, 2017.
55. A variable was created for organizational age that measures years in operation by subtracting the founding date from 2017, the year when the analysis was conducted.
56. The adjusted variance $R^2 = 0.48$, indicates that the model accounts for 48% of the variance in news nerd degree centrality.
57. The statistical insignificance of the legitimacy factors in the case study may be a result of limitations with the sample. A full discussion of the limitations of the case study sample can be found in the Appendix on Data and Methods.
58. Stinchcombe, 1965.

59. Rao et al., 2003.
60. The baseline model here is as follows: $P(Y) = 1/[1 + e^{-b_0 + b_i x_i}]$ where Y represents the probability of a news nerd and predicted by X_1, which is the combination of all legitimacy and experience variables. Leech et al., 2011.
61. The model is significant at $\chi^2 = 959.08$, $df = 21$, $p < .001$. The model explains 80% (Nagelkerke's pseudo R^2) of the variance in news nerds and correctly classifies 98% of journalists.
62. As a validity marker, this echoes findings from a survey of news nerds conducted by OpenNews (discussed further in Chapter 5), which finds that about 28% of respondents had an undergraduate degree in journalism and about 21% of respondents had a graduate degree in journalism. Findings from the survey are publicly available here https://docs.goo gle.com/spreadsheets/d/1hBmHTQGo0dAXZqEd3qWk4lz3kwKnQKhVWAqPzSHf WFs/edit#gid=1171894905
63. Wilhoit & Weaver, 2014.
64. Weaver et al., 2007.
65. Shoemaker & Vos, 2009.
66. Kreiss & Saffer, 2017. See also de Vaan et al., 2015.
67. Crossland et al., 2014.
68. Anonymous, 2017, personal communication.
69. Wei, July 6, 2017, personal communication.
70. Anonymous, 2017, personal communication.

Chapter 5

1. Schallom, 2017, personal communication.
2. Schallom, 2017, personal communication.
3. Schallom, 2017, personal communication.
4. Sulzberger, 2014, p. 91.
5. Sulzberger, 2014, p. 91.
6. Sulzberger, 2014, p. 91.
7. Leonhardt et al., 2017.
8. Baquet & Kahn, 2017, p. 4.
9. Benton, 2014, p. 5.
10. WashPostPR, 2017.
11. Silver, 2014, p. 1.
12. Clark, 2014.
13. Schallom, 2017, personal communication.
14. Anonymous, 2017, personal communication.
15. Schallom, 2017, personal communication.
16. Howard, 2014. p. 16.
17. Howard, 2014. p. 44.
18. Clark, 2014.
19. Fitts, 2014, p. 1.
20. DiMaggio & Powell, 1983.
21. Meyer & Rowan, 1977.
22. Gillin, 2013, p. 3.
23. Engelberg et al., 2018.
24. Wei, 2017, personal communication.
25. Engelberg et al., 2018.
26. Bowers, 2019, personal communication.
27. Fisher, 2019, personal communication.
28. Hepworth, 2016.
29. Stencel & Perry, 2016.

30. Rafaeli & Oliver, 1998; Zhou, 1996.
31. Massey, 2010.
32. Young & Carson, 2018.
33. As part of the data-sharing agreement, identifying information from the job database has been kept confidential.
34. Fisher, 2019, personal communication.
35. Howard, 2014, p. 46.
36. Slobin, 2017, personal communication.
37. Bell 2016. p. 4.
38. Fisher, 2019, personal communication.
39. Rahman, 2015, p. 114.
40. Chang, 2017, personal communication.
41. Medley, 2017, personal communication.
42. Chang, 2017, personal communication.
43. Anonymous news nerd, 2017, personal communication.
44. Mayes, 2019, personal communication.
45. Boyer, 2017, personal communication.
46. Wolfe, 2017, personal communication.
47. Anonymous news nerd, 2017, personal communication.
48. Mayes, 2019, personal communication.
49. Anonymous news nerd, 2017, personal communication.
50. Wolfe, 2017, personal communication.
51. Schallom, 2017, personal communication.
52. Mayes, 2019, personal communication.
53. Mayes, 2019, personal communication.
54. Lichterman, 2017.
55. Results of the 2016 OpenNews News Nerd survey can be found at https://docs.google.com/spreadsheets/d/12KWdyqrJ9vmEwHBO7zhU1V9H5m_pgvq6b1FgWWdT4Go/edit#gid=1390922297
56. Owens, 2017.
57. Results of the 2017 OpenNews News Nerd survey can be found at https://docs.google.com/spreadsheets/d/1hBmHTQGo0dAXZqEd3qWk4lz3kwKnQKhVWAqPzSHfWFs/edit#gid=1171894905

Chapter 6

1. Bowers, 2019, personal communication.
2. Tolbert & Zucker, 1996.
3. Greenwood et al., 2002.
4. Bowers, 2019, personal communication.
5. Mayes, 2019, personal communication.
6. Fisher, 2019, personal communication.
7. Welsh, 2020, personal communication.
8. Chang, 2017, personal communication.
9. Posetti, 2018, p. 7.
10. Welsh, 2020, personal communication.
11. This is similar to the way photojournalists joined news organizations, and while they raised awareness about the importance of visual modes of storytelling and the possibilities of technology in newswork, they were not great in number as the bulk of journalists still needed to write words.
12. Lowrey, 2012.
13. Micelotta et al., 2017.
14. Kosterich & Napoli, 2016.

15. Taleb, 2007.
16. Nussbaum, 2009.
17. Bowers, 2019, personal communication.
18. Lowrey, 2002.
19. Lowrey, 2002.
20. Ahuja, 2019.
21. OpenNews, which as you can recall from Chapter 2 is a network of developers, designers, journalists, and editors working at the intersection of journalism and technology that launched in 2011, set out to better understand the news nerd community in partnership with Google News Lab. The 2017 survey, named "News Nerd Survey," had 756 and public-facing results can be found here https://opennews.org/projects/2017-newsnerd-survey/.
22. https://opennews.org/projects/2017-newsnerd-survey/.
23. Bowers, 2019, personal communication.
24. https://opennews.org/projects/2017-newsnerd-survey/.
25. Sylvie, 2018.
26. Sylvie, 2018.
27. Cherubini, 2017.
28. Deuze & Steward, 2011.
29. Bilton, 2011.
30. Usher, 2016.
31. Hermida & Westlund, 2020.
32. Thanks to one of the book's anonymous reviewers for encouraging the inclusion of these ideas.
33. https://opennews.org/projects/2017-newsnerd-survey/.
34. https://opennews.org/projects/2017-newsnerd-survey/.

Appendix

1. Reay & Hinings, 2005.
2. Hermida & Young, 2019.
3. Brewer & Hunter, 2005.
4. Creswell, 2009.
5. Empson et al. 2013; Ramirez, 2013.
6. Silge & Robinson, 2016.
7. R Core Team, 2020.
8. Weber & Kosterich, 2018.
9. Nel, 2010.
10. Gulyas, 2013; Lewis & Zhong, 2013.
11. Ornebring & Mellado, 2016; Richie et al., 2003.
12. Awan, 2017.
13. Horton & Tambe, 2015.
14. Tambe, 2014.
15. Kreiss & Saffer, 2017.
16. Ge et al., 2016.
17. Ge et al., 2016.
18. Rafaeli & Oliver, 1998.
19. Zhou, 1996.
20. Massey, 2010.
21. Jick, 1979.
22. Nvivo for Windows, 2012.
23. Reay et al., 2017.
24. Gioia et al., 2013.
25. Stryker, 1996.

26. Micelotta, 2015.
27. Greenwood et al., 2002.
28. Bell, 2012.
29. Klein, 2016.
30. The case study of professional journalists in NYC is limited to 2011 through 2015 as that was the last complete year of available information at the time of data collection.
31. Monge et al., 2008.
32. Borgatti & Foster, 2003.
33. Handcock et al., 2008.
34. Handcock et al., 2008.
35. R Core Team, 2020.
36. Bastian et al., 2009.
37. Bitektine, 2011; Kennedy, 2008; Weber et al., 2016.
38. Hannan & Freeman, 1986.
39. Hanitzsch & Vos, 2017.
40. IBM Corp, 2013.
41. Leech et al., 2011.
42. Shafer & Doherty, 2017.
43. Ge et al., 2016.
44. Horton & Tambe, 2015.
45. Grant et al., 2014, p. 1201.

References

Abbott, A. (1988). *The system of professions: An essay on the division of expert labor*. Chicago, IL: University of Chicago Press.

Adler, P. S., & Kwon, S.-W. (2013). The mutation of professionalism as a contested diffusion process: Clinical guidelines as carriers of institutional change in medicine. *Journal of Management Studies, 50*(5), 930–962.

Ahuja, M. (2019). What to do when your career path is uncharted territory. Poynter. Retrieved from https://www.poynter.org/business-work/2019/cohort20/

Alikhan, A., & Thompson, K. (2015, June 15). Guardian US to launch news innovation lab focused on using mobile technology to create deeper journalism with $2.6 million from Knight Foundation. Knight Foundation. Retrieved from https://www.knightfoundation. org/press/releases/guardian-us-launch-news-innovation-lab-focused-usi

Allison, M. (1986). A literature review of approaches to the professionalism of journalists. *Journal of Mass Media Ethics, 1*(2), 5–19.

Anand, N., & Watson, M. R. (2004). Tournament rituals in the evolution of fields: The case of the Grammy Awards. *Academy of Management Journal, 47*(1), 59–80.

Ananny, M., & Crawford, K. (2015). A liminal press: Situating news app designers within a field of networked news production. *Digital Journalism, 3*(2), 192–208. doi:10.1080/ 21670811.2014.922322

Anderson, C. W. (2011). Between creative and quantified audiences: Web metrics and changing patterns of newswork in local US newsrooms. *Journalism, 12*(5), 550–566. doi:10.1177/ 1464884911402451

Anderson, C. W. (2018). *Apostles of certainty: Data journalism and the politics of doubt*. Oxford, UK: Oxford University Press.

Anderson, C. W., Bell, E., & Shirky, C. (2014). Post-industrial journalism: Adapting to the present. Tow Center for Digital Journalism at Columbia University. Retrieved from http://towcenter. org/wp-content/uploads/2012/11/TOWCenter-Post_Industrial_Journalism.pdf

Astroff, R. J. (1988). Spanish gold: Stereotypes, ideology, and the construction of a US Latino market. *Howard Journal of Communications, 1*(4), 155–173.

Awan, A. (2017, April 24). The power of LinkedIn's 500 million community. LinkedIn Official blog. Retrieved from https://blog.linkedin.com/2017/april/24/the-power-of-linkedins-500-million-community

Baquet, D., & Kahn, J. (2017, January 17). From Dean Baquet and Joe Kahn: The year ahead. *The New York Times*. Retrieved from http://www.nytco.com/from-dean-and-joe-the-year-ahead/

Barthel, M. (2017, June 1). Newspapers fact sheet. Pew Research Center. Retrieved from http:// www.journalism.org/fact-sheet/newspapers/

Barthel, M. (2018). Newspapers fact sheet. Pew Research Center. Retrieved from https://www.journalism.org/fact-sheet/newspapers/

Barthel, M., Matsa, K. E., & Worden, K. (2020). Coronavirus-driven downturn hits newspapers hard as TV news thrives. *Pew Research Center*. Retrieved from https://www.journalism.org/2020/10/29/coronavirus-driven-downturn-hits-newspapers-hard-as-tv-news-thrives/

Bastian, M., Heymann, S., & Jacomy, M. (2009). *Gephi: An open source software for exploring and manipulating networks. Proceedings of the International AAAI Conference on Web and Social Media, 3*(1), 361–362. Retrieved from https://ojs.aaai.org/index.php/ICWSM/article/view/13937.

Belair-Gagnon, V., & Holton, A. E. (2018). Boundary work, interloper media, and analytics in newsrooms. *Digital Journalism, 6*(4), 492–508.

Bell, E. (2012). Journalism by number. Columbia Journalism Review. Retrieved from http://archives.cjr.org/cover_story/journalism_by_numbers.php

Bell, E. (2015a). The rise of mobile and social news—and what it means for journalism. Reuters Institute for the Study of Journalism. Retrieved from http://www.digitalnewsreport.org/essays/2015/the-rise-of-mobile-and-social-news/

Bell, M. (2015b, February 2015). What is data journalism? Vox. Retrieved from https://www.vox.com/2015/2/4/7975535/what-is-data-journalism

Bell, E. (2016, Fall/Winter). The tech/editorial culture clash. Columbia Journalism Review. Retrieved from https://www.cjr.org/analysis/tech_editorial_facebook.php

Bell, E., Owen, T., Brown, P., Hauka, C., & Rashidian, N. (2017). The platform press: How Silicon Valley reengineered journalism. Tow Center for Digital Journalism at Columbia University. Retrieved from https://www.cjr.org/tow_center_reports/platform-press-how-silicon-valley-reengineered-journalism.php

Benes, R. (2016, October 21). Why newsrooms are expanding their data teams. Digiday. Retrieved from https://digiday.com/media/newsrooms-expanding-data-teams/

Benton, J. (2012, November 8). Luring developers into the newsroom: A new class of Knight-Mozilla fellows tries to bridge a cultural divide. Nieman Lab. Retrieved from http://www.niemanlab.org/2012/11/luring-developers-into-the-newsroom-a-new-class-of-knight-mozilla-fellows-tries-to-bridge-a-cultural-divide/

Benton, J. (2014, March 26). Columbia's Year Zero, aiming to give journalists literacy in data, is now called the Lede Program. Nieman Lab. Retrieved from http://www.niemanlab.org/2014/03/columbias-year-zero-aiming-to-give-journalists-literacy-in-data-is-now-called-the-lede-program/

Berret, C., & Phillips, C. (2016). Teaching data and computational journalism. Columbia Journalism School. Retrieved from https://journalism.columbia.edu/system/files/content/teaching_data_and_computational_journalism.pdf

Betrand, I., & Hughes, P. (2005). *Media research methods: Audiences, institutions, texts.* New York, NY: Palgrave Macmillan.

Bilton, C. (2011). The management of the creative industries from content to context. In M. Deuze (Ed.), *Managing media work* (pp. 31–42). Los Angeles, CA: SAGE.

Bilton, R. (2015, April 21). FiveThirtyEight vs. The Upshot: Who's winning the data journalism war. Digiday. Retrieved from https://digiday.com/media/fivethirtyeight-vs-upshot-whos-winning-data-journalism-war/

Bitektine, A. (2011). Toward a theory of social judgements of organizations: The case of legitimacy, reputation, and status. *Academy of Management Review, 36*(1), 151–179.

Boczkowski, P. J. (2004). *Digitizing the news: Innovation in online newspapers.* Cambridge, MA; London, UK: MIT.

Borgatti, S. P., & Foster, P. C. (2003). The network paradigm in organizational research: A review and typology. *Journal of Management, 29*(6), 991–1013.

Bowers, J. (2011, July 20). 5 steps for building a successful news app team. Poynter. Retrieved from http://www.poynter.org/2011/5-steps-for-successfully-building-a-news-app-team/139308/

Boyles, J. L. (2016). The isolation of innovation: Restructuring the digital newsroom through intrapreneurship. *Digital Journalism, 4*(2), 229–246.

Brewer, J., & Hunter, A. (2005). *Multimethod research: Synthesizing styles.* Thousand Oaks, CA: Sage.

Bunce, M. (2015). Africa in the clickstream. *African Journalism Studies, 36*(4), 12–29.

Campbell, M. J. (2006). Multiple linear regression. In *Statistics at square two: Understanding modern statistical applications in medicine* (Second ed., pp. 10–31). Oxford, UK: Blackwell Publishing Ltd.

Carlson, M. (2017). *Journalistic authority: Legitimating news in the digital era.* New York, NY: Columbia University Press.

Cherubini, F. (2017). The rise of bridge roles in news organizations. Nieman Lab. Retrieved from https://www.niemanlab.org/2017/12/the-rise-of-bridge-roles-in-news-organizations/

Cherven, K. (2015). *Mastering Gephi network visualization.* Birmingham, UK: Packt.

Clark, R. P. (2014, April 7). What it takes to create a new kind of journalism. Poynter. Retrieved from http://www.poynter.org/2014/what-it-takes-to-create-a-new-kind-of-journalism/246053/

Colyvas, J. A., & Powell, W. W. (2006). Roads to institutionalization: The remaking of boundaries between public and private science. In B. M. Staw (Ed.), *Research in organizational behavior: An annual series of analytical essays and critical reviews* (Vol. 27, pp. 305–353). New York, NY: Elsevier.

Cook, T. E. (2005). *Governing with the news: The news media as a political institution.* Chicago, IL: University of Chicago Press.

Creech, B., & Mendelson, A. L. (2015). Imagining the journalist of the future: Technological visions of journalism education and newswork. *The Communication Review, 18*, 142–165.

Creswell, J. W. (2009). *Research design: Qualitative, quantitative, and mixed methods approaches.* Thousand Oaks, CA: SAGE.

Crossland, C., Zyung, J., Hiller, N. J., & Hambrick, D. C. (2014). CEO career variety: Effects on firm-level strategic and social novelty. *Academy of Management Journal, 57*(3), 652–674.

Dacin, M. T., Goodstein, J., & Scott, W. R. (2002). Institutional theory and institutional change: Introduction to the special research forum. *Academy of Management Journal, 45*(1), 45–57.

De Vaan, M., Vedres, B., & Start, D. (2015). Game changer: The topology of creativity. *American Journal of Sociology, 120*(4), 1144–1194.

Deephouse, D. L. (1996). Does isomorphism legitimate? *The Academy of Management Journal, 39*(4), 1024–1039.

Deuze, M. (2003). The web and its journalisms: Considering the consequences of different types of news media online. *New Media & Society, 5*(2), 203–230.

Deuze, M. (2005). What is journalism? Professional identity and ideology of journalists reconsidered. *Journalism, 6*(4), 442–464.

Deuze, M., & Steward, B. (2011). Managing media work. In M. Deuze (Ed.), *Managing media work* (pp. 1–10). Los Angeles, CA: SAGE.

Dickinson, R. (2007). Accomplishing journalism: Toward a revived sociology of a media occupation. *Cultural Sociology, 1*(2), 189–206.

DiMaggio, P. J., & Powell, W. W. (1983). The iron cage revisited: Institutional isomorphism and collective rationality in organizational fields. *American Sociological Review, 48*(2), 147–160.

DiMaggio, P. J., & Powell, W. W. (1991). *The new institutionalism in organizational analysis.* Chicago, IL: University of Chicago Press.

Dixon, C. (2014, August 10). BuzzFeed. cdixon blog. Retrieved from http://cdixon.org/2014/08/10/buzzfeed/

Doctor, K. (2015, July 28). Newsonomics: The halving of America's daily newsrooms. Nieman Lab. Retrieved from http://www.niemanlab.org/2015/07/newsonomics-the-halving-of-americas-daily-newsrooms/

Dyer, J., Gregersen, H., & Christensen, C. (2011). *The innovator's DNA: Mastering the five skills of disruptive innovations*. Boston, MA: Harvard Business Review Press.

Eldridge, S. A., II. (2019). "Thank god for Deadspin": Interlopers, metajournalistic commentary, and fake news through the lens of "journalistic realization." *New Media & Society, 21*(4), 856–878.

Ellis, J. (2013, November 25). Q&A: *The Guardian's* Gabriel Dance on new tools for story and cultivating interactive journalism. Nieman Lab. Retrieved from http://www.niemanlab.org/2013/11/qa-the-guardians-gabriel-dance-on-new-tools-for-story-and-cultivating-interactive-journalism/

Empson, L., Cleaver, I., & Allen, J. (2013). Managing partners and management professionals: Institutional work dyads in professional partnerships. *Journal of Management Studies, 50*, 808–844.

Engelberg, S., Tofel, R., & Fields, R. (2018). Welcome to our second decade: Much has changed since ProPublica published its first story, but we remain committed to the power of fact-based journalism to spur change and right wrongs. ProPublica. Retrieved from https://www.propublica.org/article/propublica-10th-anniversary-welcome-to-our-second-decade

Ferrucci, P., & Vos, T. P. (2017). Who's in, who's out? Constructing the identity of digital journalists. *Digital Journalism, 5*(7), 868–883.

Finberg, H. (2014, April 9). Journalism needs the right skills to survive. Poynter. Retrieved from https://www.poynter.org/2014/journalism-needs-the-right-skills-to-survive/246563/

Fincham, K. (2012, February 7). Journalists connect the dots between data & reporting at Columbia J-school hackathon. Poynter. Retrieved from https://www.poynter.org/2012/journalists-connect-the-dots-between-data-reporting-at-columbia-j-school-hackathon/162131/

Fitts, A. S. (2014, January/February). Snow Fall vs. Snow Fail: The flashy "future" of journalism. Columbia Journalism Review. Retrieved from http://archives.cjr.org/currents/snow_fall_vs_snow_fail.php

Foster, R. (2012). News plurality in a digital world. Reuters Institute for the Study of Journalism. Retrieved from http://reutersinstitute.politics.ox.ac.uk/sites/default/files/News%20Plurality%20in%20a%20Digital%20World.pdf

Funt, D. (2014). How journalism schools are adjusting to the digital age. Columbia Journalism Review. Retrieved from http://experiment.cjr.org/experiment/features/how-journalism-schools-are-adjusting-to-the-digital-age/

Ge, C., Huang, K.-W., & Png, I. P. L. (2016). Engineer/scientist careers: Patents, online profiles, and misclassification bias. *Strategic Management Journal, 37*, 232–253.

Gillin, J. (2013, April 26). New AP interactive editor: Multimedia needs to be "central to developing the story," not an afterthought. Poynter. Retrieved from https://www.poynter.org/2013/new-ap-interactive-editor-multimedia-needs-to-be-central-to-developing-the-story-not-an-afterthought/210693/

Gioia, D. A., Corley, K. G., & Hamilton, A. L. (2013). Seeking qualitative rigor in inductive research notes on the Gioia methodology. *Organizational Research Methods, 16*(1), 15–31.

Glynn, M. A. (2008). How institutions enable identities. In R. Greenwood, C. Oliver, K. Sahlin, & R. Suddaby (Eds.), *The Sage handbook of organizational institutionalism* (pp. 413–430). Thousand Oaks, CA: SAGE.

Gordon, R. (2018). Groundbreaking journalism scholarship seeks two more software developers. Medium. Retrieved from https://medium.com/@richgor/groundbreaking-journalism-scholarship-seeks-two-more-software-developers-693589f5ea62

Grant, A. M., Berg, J. M., & Cable, D. M. (2014). Job titles as identity badges: How self-reflecting titles can reduce emotional exhaustion. *Academy of Management Journal, 57*(4), 1201–1225.

Greenwood, R., & Suddaby, R. (2006). Institutional entrepreneurship in mature fields: The big five accounting firms. *Academy of Management, 49*(1), 27–48.

Greenwood, R., Suddaby, R., & Hinings, C. R. (2002). Theorizing change: The role of professional associations in the transformation of institutionalized fields. *The Academy of Management Journal, 45*(1), 58–80.

Grieco, E. (2020). U.S. newspapers have shed half of their newsroom employees since 2008. Pew Reasearch. Retrieved from https://www.pewresearch.org/fact-tank/2020/04/20/u-s-newsroom-employment-has-dropped-by-a-quarter-since-2008/

Grueskin, B., Seave, A., & Graves, L. (2011, May 10). Chapter one: News from everywhere. Columbia Journalism Review. Retrieved from http://archives.cjr.org/the_business_of_dig ital_journalism/chapter_one_news_from_everywhere.php

Gulyas, A. (2013). The influence of professional variables on journalists' uses and views of social media: A comparative study of Finland, Germany, Sweden and the United Kingdom. *Digital Journalism, 1*(2), 270–285.

Hagel, J., III, & Brown, J. S. (2017, June 7). Great businesses scale their learning, not just their operations. *Harvard Business Review*. Retrieved from https://hbr.org/2017/06/great-bus inesses-scale-their-learning-not-just-their-operations

Hallin, D. C., & Mancini, P. (2004). *Comparing media systems: Three models of media and politics.* Cambridge, UK: Cambridge University Press.

Hamilton, J. T. (2004). *All the news that's fit to sell: How the market transforms information into news.* Princeton, NJ: Princeton University Press.

Hamilton, J. T. (2016). *Democracy's detectives: The economics of investigative journalism.* Cambridge, MA: Harvard University Press.

Handcock, M. S., Hunter, D. R., Butts, C. T., Goodreau, S. M., & Morris, M. (2008). statnet: Software tools for the representation, visualization, analysis, and simulation of network data. *Journal of Statistical Software, 24*(1).

Hanitzsch, T., & Vos, T. P. (2017). Journalistic roles and the struggle over institutional identity: The discursive constitution of journalism. *Communication Theory, 27*(2), 115–135.

Hannan, M. T., & Freeman, J. (1986). Where do organizational forms come from? *Sociological Forum, 1*(1), 50–72.

Hansen, M. L. (1976). *Exploring writing careers: A student guidebook.* Washington, D.C.: U.S. Government Printing Office.

Hanusch, F. (2016). Web analytics and the functional differentiation of journalism cultures. *Information, Communication & Society, 20*(10), 1571–1586.

Hardy, C., & Maguire, S. (2008). Institutional entrepreneurship. In R. Greenwood, C. Oliver, K. Sahlin, & R. Suddaby (Eds.), *The Sage handbook of organizational institutionalism* (pp. 198–217). Thousand Oaks, CA: SAGE.

Hare, K. (2015, September 30). With money from Knight, the AP will create standards for data journalism. Poynter. Retrieved from https://www.poynter.org/2015/with-money-from-kni ght-the-ap-will-create-standards-for-data-journalism/375934/

Hasenpusch, T. C., & Baumann, S. (2017). Strategic media venturing: Corporate venture capital approaches of TIME incumbents. *International Journal on Media Management, 19*(1), 77–100.

Haughney, C. (2013, April 15). *Times* wins four Pulitzers; Brooklyn nonprofit is awarded a reporting prize. *The New York Times*. Retrieved from http://www.nytimes.com/2013/04/16/business/media/the-times-wins-four-pulitzer-prizes.html

Hepworth, S. (2016, August 2). Exit interview: Aron Pilhofer on the digital landscape, buyouts at *The Guardian.* Columbia Journalism Review. Retrieved from https://www.cjr.org/q_and_a/aron_pilhofer_guardian_buyouts.php

Heravi, B. R. (2019). 3Ws of data journalism education: What, where and who? *Journalism Practice, 13*(3), 349–366.

Hermida, A., & Westlund, O. (2020). The virus ups data journalism's game. Neiman Lab. Retrieved from https://www.niemanlab.org/2020/12/the-virus-ups-data-journalisms-game/

Hermida, A., & Young, M. L. (2019). *Data journalism and the regeneration of news.* London, UK: Routledge.

Hickson, D. J., Hinings, C. R., Lee, C. A., Schneck, R. E., & Pennings, J. (1971). A strategic contingencies theory of intra-organizational power. *Administrative Science Quarterly, 16,* 216–229.

Holton, A. E., & Belair-Gagnon, V. (2018). Strangers to the game? Interlopers, intralopers, and shifting news production. *Media and Communication, 6*(4), 70–78.

Horton, J. J., & Tambe, P. (2015). Labor economists get their microscope: Big data and labor market analysis. *Big Data, 3*(3), 130–137.

Howard, A. B. (2014, May). The art and science of data-driven journalism. Tow Center for Digital Journalism at Columbia University. Retrieved from http://towcenter.org/wp-content/uplo ads/2014/05/Tow-Center-Data-Driven-Journalism.pdf

IBM Corp. (2013). *IBM SPSS Statistics for Windows, version 22.0.* Armonk, NY: IBM Corp.

Ingram, M. (2012, January 5). Can newspapers also be tech incubators. Gigaom. Retrieved from https://gigaom.com/2012/01/05/can-newspapers-also-be-tech-incubators/

Ivancsics, B., & Hansen, M. (2019). Acutally, it's about ethics, AI, and journalism: Reporting on and with computation and data. Tow Center for Digital Journalism at Columbia University. Retrieved from cjr.org/tow_center_reports/ai-ethics-journalism-and-computation-ibm-new-york-times.php

Jick, T. D. (1979). Mixing qualitative and quantitative methods: Triangulation in action. *Administrative Science Quarterly, 24*(4), 602–611.

Kennedy, M. T. (2008). Getting counted: Markets, media, and reality. *American Sociological Review, 73*(2), 270–295. doi:10.1177/000312240807300205

Kieser, A. (1994). Why organization theory needs historical analyses—and how this should be performed. *Organization Science, 5*(4), 608–620.

Klein, S. (2016, April 7). Want to start a small data journalism team in your newsroom? Here are 8 steps. Nieman Lab. Retrieved from http://www.niemanlab.org/2016/04/want-to-start-a-small-data-journalism-team-in-your-newsroom-here-are-8-steps/

Kosterich, A., & Napoli, P. M. (2016). Reconfiguring the audience commodity: The institutionalization of social TV analytics as market information regime. *Television & New Media, 17*(3), 254–271. doi:10.1177/1527476415597480

Kosterich, A., Saffer, A., Weber, M. S., & Kreiss, D. (in press). Network histories: New methods and measures for studying the production of communication.

Kosterich, A., & Weber, M. (2019a). Starting up the news: The impact of venture capital on the digital news media ecosystem. *International Journal on Media Management, 20*(4), 239–262. doi:10.1080/14241277.2018.1563547

Kosterich, A., & Weber, M. S. (2019b). Transformation of a modern newsroom workforce: A case study of NYC journalist network histories from 2011 to 2015. *Journalism Practice, 13*(4), 431–457. doi:10.1080/17512786.2018.1497454

Kreiss, D., & Saffer, A. J. (2017). Networks and innovation in the production of communication: Explaining innovations in U.S. electoral campaigning from 2004 to 2012. *Journal of Communication, 67*(4), 521–544.

Leblebici, H., Salancik, G. R., Copay, A., & King, T. (1991). Institutional change and the transformation of interorganizational fields: An organizational history of the U.S. radio broadcasting industry. *Administrative Science Quarterly, 36*(3), 333–363.

Lee, K., & Pennings, J. M. (2002). Mimicry and the market: Adoption of a new organizational form. *Academy of Management Journal, 45*(1), 144–162.

Leech, N. L., Barrett, K. C., & Morgan, G. A. (Eds.). (2011). *IBM SPSS for intermediate statistics: Use and interpretation* (5th ed.). New York, NY: Routledge.

Leicht, K. T., & Fennell, M. L. (2008). Institutionalism and the professions. In R. Greenwood, C. Oliver, K. Sahlin, & R. Suddaby (Eds.), *The Sage handbook of organizational institutionalism* (pp. 431–448). Thousand Oaks, CA: SAGE.

Leonhardt, David, Rudoren, Jodi, Galinsky, Jon, Skog, Karron, Lacey, Marc, Giratikanon, Tom, & Evans, Tyson. (2017). Journalism that stands apart: The report of the 2020 group. *The New York Times.* Retrieved from https://www.nytimes.com/projects/2020-report/

Lewis, N., & Zhong, B. (2013). The root of journalistic plagiarism: Contested attribution beliefs. *Journalism & Mass Communication Quarterly, 90*(1), 148–166.

Lewis, S. C., & Usher, N. (2013). Open source and journalism: Toward new frameworks for imagining news innovation. *Media Culture & Society, 35*(5), 602–619. doi:10.1177/0163443713485494

Lewis, S. C., & Westlund, O. (2015a). Actors, actants, audiences, and activities in cross-media news work. *Digital Journalism, 3*(1), 19–37.

Lewis, S. C., & Westlund, O. (2015b). Journalism in an era of big data: Cases, concepts, and critiques. *Digital Journalism, 3*(3), 447–466.

Lewis, S. C., & Westlund, O. (2016). Mapping the human-machine divide in journalism. In T. Witschge, C. W. Anderson, D. Domingo, & A. Hermida (Eds.), *The Sage handbook of digital journalism* (pp. 341–353). Thousand Oaks, CA: SAGE.

Li, A. (2013, September 13). Online course shows impact, importance of data-driven journalism. Poynter. Retrieved from http://www.poynter.org/2013/online-course-shows-impact-importance-of-data-driven-journalism/223548/

Lichterman, J. (2017, March 2). A new OpenNews survey creates a "baseline for what we can do to broaden" the news nerd community. Nieman Lab. Retrieved from http://www.niemanlab.org/2017/03/a-new-opennews-survey-creates-a-baseline-for-what-we-can-do-to-broaden-the-news-nerd-community/

Lowrey, W. (2002). Word people vs. picture people: Normative differences and strategies for control over work among newsroom subgroups. *Mass Communication & Society, 5*(4), 411–432.

Lowrey, W. (2011). Institutionalism, news organizations and innovation. *Journalism Studies, 12*(1), 64–79.

Lowrey, W. (2012). Journalism innovation and the ecology of news production: Institutional tendencies. *Journalism and Communication Monographs, 14,* 214–287. doi:10.1177/1522637912463207

Lynch, D. (2015). Above & beyond: Looking at the future of journalism education. Knight Foundation. Retrieved from https://www.knightfoundation.org/features/journalism-education/

Maguire, S., Hardy, C., & Lawrence, T. B. (2004). Institutional entrepreneurship in emerging fields: HIV/AIDS treatment advocacy in Canada. *Academy of Management Journal, 47,* 657–679.

Marquis, C., & Lounsbury, M. (2007). Vive la resistance: Competing logics and the consolidation of US community banking. *Academy of Management Journal, 50*(4), 799–820.

Massey, B. L. (2010). What job advertisements tell us about demand for multiplatform reporters at legacy news outlets. *Journalism & Mass Communication Educator, 65*(2), 142–155.

McDonald, L. (2019). How BuzzFeed's Tech Team helps journalists report on technology with authority. BuzzFeed Tech. Retrieved from https://tech.buzzfeed.com/tech-and-news-working-group-7dabaaa38e45

McKenzie, H. (2013, February 14). Disruption from the inside: Media companies seek hope in incubators. Pando. Retrieved from https://pando.com/2013/02/14/disruption-from-the-inside-media-companies-seek-hope-in-incubators/

Medill School of Journalism. (2007, June 9). Medill offers journalism scholarships to programmer/developers. Northwestern University. Retrieved from https://web.archive.org/web/20070609150000/http://www.medill.northwestern.edu/medill/admissions/programmers.html

Meyer, A. D., Brooks, G. R., & Goes, J. B. (1990). Environmental jolts and industry revolutions: Organizational responses to discontinuous change. *Strategic Management Journal, 11*(1), 93–110.

Meyer, J. W., & Rowan, B. (1977). Institutional organizations: Structure as myth and ceremony. *American Journal of Sociology, 83*(2), 340–363.

Meyer, P. (1973). *Precision journalism: A reporter's introduction to social science methods.* Lanham, MD: Rowman & Littlefield.

Micelotta, E., Lounsbury, M., & Greenwood, R. (2017). Pathways of institutional change: An integrative review and research agenda. *Journal of Management, 43*(6), 1–26.

Micelotta, E. R. (2015). *When institutions bend but do not break: The institutional accommodation of Open Access in scientific publishing.* (PhD diss.) University of Alberta, Canada.

Mitchell, A., & Page, D. (2014). State of the news media 2014: Growth in digital reporting: What it means for journalism and news consumers. Pew Research Center. Retrieved from http://www.journalism.org/files/2014/03/Shifts-in-Reporting_For-uploading.pdf

Monge, P., Heiss, B., & Margolin, D. (2008). Communication network evolution in organizational communities. *Communication Theory, 18*(4), 449–477.

Morrison, S. (2014, July). The toy department shall lead us. Columbia Journalism Review. Retrieved from http://archives.cjr.org/reports/the_toy_department_shall_lead.php

Moses, L. (2014, June 16). "Employee of the future": Bridging media's church and state divide. Digiday. Retrieved from https://digiday.com/media/meet-new-hybrid-publishing-employees-mix-edit-business/

Muzio, D., Brock, D. M., & Suddaby, R. (2013). Professions and institutional change: Towards an institutionalist sociology of the professions. *Journal of Management Studies, 50*(5), 699–721.

Myers, S. (2011, February 17). Key departures suggest 4 factors critical to the future of programming and journalism. Poynter. Retrieved from http://www.poynter.org/2011/key-departures-point-to-4-factors-critical-to-the-future-of-programming-and-journalism/119853/

Naldi, L., & Picard, R. G. (2012). "Let's start an online news site": Opportunities, resources, strategy, and formational myopia in startups. *Journal of Media Business Studies, 9*(4), 69–97.

Neheli, N. B. (2018). News by numbers. *Digital Journalism, 6*(8), 1041–1051.

Nel, F. (2010, August 14). Updated: How many journalists are there in the UK? This is why I guestimate around 40,000 (that's more than a third less than the number often quoted). For the Media blog. Retrieved from http://forthemedia.blogspot.co.uk/2010/08/how-journalists-are-there-in-uk-this-is.html

Newman, N., Fletcher, R., Schulz, A., Andi, S., & Nielsen, R. K. (2020). Reuters Institute digital news report 2020. Reuters Institute for Study of Jouranlism. Retrieved from https://reutersinstitute.politics.ox.ac.uk/sites/default/files/2020-06/DNR_2020_FINAL.pdf

Nussbaum, E. (2009, January 2009). The new journalism: Goosing the Gray Lady. *New York Magazine.* Retrieved from http://nymag.com/news/features/all-new/53344/

Nvivo for Windows. (2012). NVivo qualitative data analysis Software: QSR International Pty Ltd.

O'Donovan, C. (2014, May 14). NowThis News, a leader in mobile/social/video, shifts its strategy and its personnel. Nieman Lab. Retrieved from http://www.niemanlab.org/2014/05/nowthis-news-a-leader-in-mobilesocialvideo-shifts-its-strategy-and-its-personnel/

Ognyanova, K. (2016). Network analysis and visualization with R and igraph. *Katya Ognyanova.* Retrieved from http://www.kateto.net/wp-content/uploads/2016/01/NetSciX_2016_Workshop.pdf]

OJA. (2015). Excellence and innovation in visual digital storytelling. Online News Association. Retrieved from https://awards.journalists.org/awards/visual-digital-storytelling/page/2/

OpenNews. (2017). Meet the Knight-Mozilla Fellowship community. OpenNews blog. Retrieved from https://opennews.org/what/fellowships/community/

Oputu, E. (2014, April 8). WNYC is beefing up its data journalism. Columbia Journalism Review. Retrieved from http://archives.cjr.org/behind_the_news/wnyc_is_beefing_up_its_data_jo.php

Ornebring, H. (2009). The two professionalisms of journalism: Journalism and the changing context of work. Reuters Institute for the Study of Journalism (Working Paper). Retrieved from https://reutersinstitute.politics.ox.ac.uk/sites/default/files/The%20Two%20Professionalisms%20of%20Journalism_Working%20Paper_0.pdf

Ornebring, H., & Mellado, C. (2016). Valued skills among journalists: An exploratory comparison of six European nations. *Journalism, 19*(4), 445–463.

Owens, E. (2017, March 2). Who are the news nerds? OpenNews. Retrieved from https://opennews.org/blog/news-nerd-survey/

Parasie, S., & Dagiral, E. (2012). Data-driven journalism and the public good: "Computer-assisted-reporters" and "programmer-journalists" in Chicago. *New Media & Society, 15*(6), 853–871.

Peters, M. (2012, July 27). Why social media roles in newsrooms shouldn't just be for "young people." Poynter. Retrieved from http://www.poynter.org/2012/why-social-media-roles-in-newsrooms-shouldnt-just-be-for-young-people/182919/

Petre, C. (2015, May). The traffic factories: Metrics at Chartbeat, Gawker Media, and the *New York Times*. Tow Center for Digital Journalism at Columbia University. Retrieved from https://www.cjr.org/tow_center_reports/the_traffic_factories_metrics_at_chartbeat_gawker_media_and_the_new_york_times.php

Pfeffer, J., & Salancik, G. R. (1978). *The external control of organizations: A resource dependence perspective*. New York, NY: Harper & Row.

Polgreen, E. (2014, November 5). Why in-house innovation is a great plan for legacy outlets. Columbia Journalism Review. Retrieved from https://www.cjr.org/innovations/intrapreneurship.php

Pollack, T. G., & Rindova, V. P. (2003). Media legitimation effects in the market for initial public offerings. *Academy of Management Journal, 46*(5), 631–642.

Posetti, J. (2018). Time to step away from the "bright, shiny things"? Towards a sustainable model of journalism innovation in an era of perpetual change. *Reuters Institute for the Study of Journalism*. Retrieved from https://reutersinstitute.politics.ox.ac.uk/sites/default/files/2018-11/Posetti_Towards_a_Sustainable_model_of_Journalism_FINAL.pdf

Powell, W. W., & DiMaggio, P. J. (1991). *The new institutionalism in organizational analysis*. Chicago, IL: University of Chicago Press.

Powers, M. (2012). "In forms that are familiar and yet-to-be invented": American journalism and the discourse of technologically specific work. *Journal of Communication Inquiry, 36*(1), 24–43.

PrivCo. (2017). BuzzFeed, Inc.: Private company financial report. PrivCo database. Retrieved from http://www.privco.com/private-company/buzzfeed-inc

R Core Team. (2020). R: A language and environment for statistical computing. *R-project for statistical computing*. Retrieved from www.R-project.org

Rafaeli, A., & Oliver, A. L. (1998). Employment ads: A configurational research agenda. *Journal of Management Inquiry, 7*(4), 342–358.

Rahman, Z. (2015). So you found a unicorn—what now? In T. Felle, J. Mair, & D. Radcliffe (Eds.), *Data journalism: Inside the global future* (pp. 112–117). Suffolk, UK: Abramis Academic.

Ramirez, C. (2013). "We are being pilloried for something we did not even know we had done wrong!" Quality control and orders of worth in the British audit profession. *Journal of Management Studies, 50*, 845–869.

Rao, H., Monin, P., & Durand, R. (2003). Institutional change in Toque Ville: Nouvelle cuisine as an identity movement in French gastronomy. *American Journal of Sociology, 108*(4), 795–843.

Rashidian, N., Civeris, G., Brown, P., Bell, E., & Hartstone, A. (2019). Platforms and publishers: The end of an era. Tow Center for Digital Journalism at Columbia University. Retrieved from https://www.cjr.org/tow_center_reports/platforms-and-publishers-end-of-an-era.php

Reay, T., Goodrick, E., Waldorff, S. B., & Casebeer, A. (2017). Getting leopards to change their spots: Co-creating a new professional role identity. *Academy of Management Journal, 60*(3), 1043–1070.

Reay, T., & Hinings, C. R. (2005). The recomposition of an organizational field: Health care in Alberta. *Organization Studies, 26*(3), 351–384.

Redohl, S. (2017, May 17). Excellence in immersive storytelling a new category in ONA's 2017 online journalism awards. Immersive Shooter. Retrieved from http://www.immersiveshooter.com/2017/05/17/excellence-in-immersive-storytelling-new-category-ona-2017-online-journalism-awards/?utm_content=buffer7d77d&utm_medium=social&utm_source=twitter.com&utm_campaign=buffer

Richie, J., Lewis, J., & Elam, G. (2003). Designing and selecting samples. In J. Richie & J. Lewis (Eds.), *Qualitative research methods: A guide for social science researchers and students* (pp. 77–108). London, UK: SAGE.

Romenesko, J. (2012, December 27). More than 3.5 million page views for *New York Times'* "Snow Fall" feature. Jimromenesko.com. Retrieved from http://jimromenesko.com/2012/12/27/more-than-3-5-million-page-views-for-nyts-snow-fall/

Ryfe, D. M. (2012). *Can journalism survive? An inside look at American newsrooms.* Cambridge, MA: Polity Press.

Ryley, J. (2021). The pandemic has put data journalism to the test and shown us that facts and figures can bring news to life. *Sky.* Retrieved from https://www.skygroup.sky/article/the-pandemic-has-put-data-journalism-to-the-test-and-shown-us-that-facts-and-figu res-can-bring-news-to-life_

Schudson, M. (2002). The news media as political institutions. *Annual Review of Political Science, 5,* 239–269.

Scott, W. R. (1995). *Institutions and organizations.* Thousand Oaks, CA: SAGE.

Scott, W. R. (2001). *Institutions and organizations* (2nd ed.). Thousand Oaks, CA: SAGE.

Shafer, J., & Doherty, T. (2017, May/June). The media bubble is worse than you think. *Politico.* Retrieved from http://www.politico.com/magazine/story/2017/04/25/media-bubble-real-journalism-jobs-east-coast-215048.

Shoemaker, P. J., & Vos, T. P. (2009). *Gatekeeping theory.* New York, NY: Routledge.

Silge, J., & Robinson, D. (2016). tidytext: Text mining and analysis using tidy data principles in R. *JOSS, 1*(3). doi:10.21105/joss.00037

Silver, N. (2014, January 27). Status update: Building FiveThirtyEight. FiveThirtyEight. Retrieved from https://fivethirtyeight.com/features/status-update-building-fivethirtyeight/

Singer, J. B. (2003). Who are these guys? The online challenge to the notion of journalistic professionalism. *Journalism, 4*(2), 139–163.

Slack, T., & Hinings, B. (1994). Institutional pressures and isomorphic change: An empirical test. *Organization Studies, 15*(6), 803–827.

Smets, M., Morris, T., & Greenwood, R. (2012). From practice to field: A multilevel model of practice-driven institutional change. *Academy of Management Journal, 55*(4), 877–904.

Spinner, J. (2014, September 24). The big conundrum: Should journalists learn to code? American Journalism Review. Retrieved from http://ajr.org/2014/09/24/should-journali sts-learn-code/

Splendore, S., Salvo, P. D., Eberwein, T., Groenhart, H., Just, M., & Porlezza, C. (2016). Educational strategies in data journalism: A comparative study of six European countries. *Journalism, 17*(1), 138–152.

Stencel, M., & Perry, K. (2016). Superpowers: The digital skills media leaders say newsrooms need going forward. Tow-Knight Center for Entrepreneurial Journalism at CUNY Graduate School of Journalism. Retrieved from http://towknight.org/research/superpowers/

Stinchcombe, A. L. (1965). Organizations and social structure. In J. March (Ed.), *Handbook of organizations* (pp. 153–193). Chicago, IL: Rand McNally.

Stray, J. (2012, October 31). Data, uncertainty, and specialization: What journalism can learn from FiveThirtyEight's election coverage. Nieman Lab. Retrieved from http://www.nieman lab.org/2012/10/data-uncertainty-and-specialization-what-journalism-can-learn-from-fivethirtyeights-election-coverage/

Stryker, R. (1996). Beyond history versus theory: Strategic narrative and sociological explanation. *Sociological Methods & Research, 24*(3), 304–502.

Suchman, M. C. (1995). Managing legitimacy: Strategic and institutional approaches. *Academy of Management Review, 20*(3), 517–610.

Sulzberger, A. (2014). *New York Times* Innovation Report. Scribd. Retrieved from https://www.scribd.com/doc/224332847/NYT-Innovation-Report-2014

Sylvie, G. (2018). *Reshaping the news: Community, engagement, and editors.* New York, NY: Peter Lang.

Symposium on Computation + Journalism. (2008). Journalism 3G: The future of technology in the field. Georgia Institute of Technology. Retrieved from http://www.computation-and-journalism.com/symposium2008/

Taleb, N. N. (2007). *The black swan: The impact of the highly improbable*. New York, NY: Random House.

Tambe, P. (2014). Big data investment, skills, and firm value. *Management Science, 60*(6), 1452–1469.

Tandoc, Edson C., Jr. (2019). Journalism at the periphery. *Media and Communication, 7*(4), 138–143.

Thomas, J. (2011, August 29). Meet the young designer behind *The Washington Post*'s infographics. *Forbes*. Retrieved from https://www.forbes.com/sites/jessethomas/2011/08/29/meet-the-young-designer-behind-the-washington-posts-infographics/#1630bca15aa8

Thompson, B. (2014, August 12). Is Buzzfeed a tech company? Stratechery. Retrieved from https://stratechery.com/2014/buzzfeed-tech-company/

Tolbert, P. S., & Zucker, L. G. (1996). The institutionalization of institutional theory. In S. R. Clegg, C. Hardy, & W. R. Nord (Eds.), *Handbook of organization studies* (pp. 175–190). Thousand Oaks, CA: SAGE.

Tourino, A. C. (2017). *Nerd journalism: How data and digital technology transformed news graphics*. (PhD diss.) Barcelona, Spain: Uniersitat Oberta de Catalunya.

Tushman, M. L., & Anderson, P. (1986). Technological discontinuties and organizational environments. *Administrative Science Quarterly, 31*(3), 439–465.

Uberti, D. (2014, September 1). How robots consumed journalism. Columbia Journalism Review. Retrieved from http://archives.cjr.org/currents/robot_journalism.php

Usher, N. (2013). Al Jazeera English online: Understanding web metrics and news production when a quantified audience is not a commodified audience. *Digital Journalism, 1*(3), 335–351.

Usher, N. (2016). *Interactive journalism: Hackers, data, and code*. Champaign, IL: University of Illinois Press.

Usher, N. (2017). Venture-backed news startups and the field of journalism: Challenges, changes, and consistencies. *Digital Journalism, 5*(9), 1116–1133.

Waite, M. (2011, March 8). Matt Waite: To build a digital future for news, developers must be able to hack at the core of old systems. Nieman Lab. Retrieved from http://www.niemanlab.org/2011/03/matt-waite-to-build-a-digital-future-for-news-developers-have-to-be-able-to-hack-at-the-core-of-the-old-ways/

Walker, M. (2019). Americans favor mobile devices over desktops and laptops for getting news. Pew Research Center. Retrieved from https://www.pewresearch.org/fact-tank/2019/11/19/americans-favor-mobile-devices-over-desktops-and-laptops-for-getting-news/

WashPost PR. (2017). The *Post* announces three new roles to standardize digital responsibilities in the newsroom. WashPost PR blog. Retrieved from https://www.washingtonpost.com/pr/wp/2017/08/18/the-post-announces-three-new-roles-to-standardize-digital-responsibilities-in-the-newsroom/

Wasserman, S., & Faust, K. (1994). *Social network analysis: Methods and applications*. Cambridge, UK: Cambridge University Press.

Weaver, D. H., Beam, R. A., Brownlee, B. J., Voakes, P. S., & Wilhoit, G. C. (2007). *The American journalist in the 21st century: U.S. news people at the dawn of a new millennium*. New York, NY: Lawrence Erlbaum.

Weber, H. (2013, January 29). The *NY Times* announces timeSpace: A 4 month incubator for early stage media startups. The Next Web. Retrieved from https://thenextweb.com/media/2013/01/29/the-ny-times-announces-timespace-a-4-month-incubator-for-early-stage-media-startups/#.tnw_MGmZjFAR

Weber, M. S., Fulk, J., & Monge, P. (2016). The emergence and evolution of social networking sites as an organizational form. *Management Communication Quarterly, 30*(3), 305–332.

Weber, M. S., & Kosterich, A. (2018). Managing a 21st-century newsroom workforce: A case study of NYC news media. Tow Center for Digital Journalism at Columbia University. Retrieved from https://www.cjr.org/tow_center_reports/managing-a-newsroom-workforce-nyc-case-study.php/

Wenzel, A. (2017, May 25). Lessons in audience engagement from Chicago's Curious City. Columbia Journalism Review. Retrieved from https://www.cjr.org/tow_center/lessons-in-audience-engagement-from-chicagos-curious-city.php

Wickenden, M. T. (1991). *A day in the life of a newspaper reporter*. Mahwah, NJ: Troll Associates.

Wilhoit, L., & Weaver, D. H. (2014). The American journalist in the digital age: Key findings. School of Journalism, Indiana University. Retrieved from https://larswillnat.files.wordpress.com/2014/05/2013-american-journalist-key-findings.pdf

Williams, W., & Martin, F. L. (1911). *The practice of journalism, a treatise on newspaper making*. Columbia, MO: E.W. Stephens.

Wright, A., Zammuto, R. F., & Liesch, P. W. (2017). Maintaining the values of a profession: Institutional work and moral emotions in the emergency department. *Academy of Management Journal, 60*(1), 200–237.

Wu, L. (2016). Did you get the buzz? Are digital native media becoming mainstream? . *#ISOJ, 6*(1). Retrieved from https://isojjournal.wordpress.com/2016/04/14/did-you-get-the-buzz-are-digital-native-media-becoming-mainstream/

Young, S., & Carson, A. (2018). What is a journalist? *Journalism Studies, 19*(3), 452–472.

Zamith, R. (2019). Transparency, interactivity, diversity, and information provenance in everyday data journalism. *Digital Journalism, 7*(4), 470–489.

Zelizer, B. (1995). Journalism's "last" stand: Wirephoto and the discourse of resistance. *Journal of Communication, 45*(2), 78–92.

Zhou, Y. (1996). Analysis of trends in demand for computer-related skills for academic librarians from 1974 to 1994. *College & Research Libraries, 57*, 259–272.

Index

For the benefit of digital users, indexed terms that span two pages (e.g., 52–53) may, on occasion, appear on only one of those pages.

Tables and figures are indicated by *t* and *f* following the page number

Printed in the USA/Agawam, MA
November 11, 2022

801102.030